C4

D1326927

TITANIC LOVE STORIES

The true stories of 13 honeymoon couples
who sailed on the Titanic

GILL PAUL

Ivy Press

To Karel

★

First published in the UK in 2011 by
Ivy Press
210 High Street
Lewes
East Sussex BN7 2NS
United Kingdom
www.ivy-group.co.uk

Copyright © Ivy Press Limited 2011

All rights reserved. No part of this book may be reproduced or transmitted
in any form or by any means, electronic or mechanical, including photocopying,
recording, or by any information storage-and-retrieval system, without
written permission from the copyright holder.

British Library Cataloguing-in-Publication Data
A catalogue record for this book is available from the British Library

ISBN: 978-1-907332-78-4

Ivy Press

This book was conceived, designed and produced by Ivy Press

Creative Director Peter Bridgewater

Publisher Jason Hook

Art Director Wayne Blades

Senior Editor Jayne Ansell

Designer Andrew Milne

Picture Researcher Shelley Noronha

Newcastle Libraries & Information Service	
C4 666397 00 17	
Askews & Holts	Feb-2012
363.123	£14.99

Contents

WHITE STAR LINE

ROYAL & STEAMERS
UNITED STATES MAIL

FIRST SAILING OF THE LATEST ADDITION TO THE WHITE STAR FLEET

The Queen of the Ocean

TITANIC

LENGTH 882½ FT.   OVER 45,000 TONS   BEAM 92½ FT.
TRIPLE-SCREWS

This, the Latest, Largest and Finest Steamer Afloat, will sail from
WHITE STAR LINE, PIER 59 (North River), NEW YORK

Saturday, April 20th   At 12 Noon

THIRD CLASS FOUR BERTH ROOM

Spacious Dining Saloons
Smoking Room
Ladies' Reading Room
Covered Promenade

All passengers berthed in closed rooms containing 2, 4, or 6 berths, a large number equipped with washstands, etc.

THIRD CLASS DINING SALOON

Reservations of Berths may be made direct with this Office or through any of our accredited Agents

THIRD CLASS RATES ARE:

To PLYMOUTH, SOUTHAMPTON, LONDON, LIVERPOOL and GLASGOW,	$36.25
To GOTHENBURG, MALMÖ, CHRISTIANIA, COPENHAGEN, ESBJERG, Etc.	41.50
To STOCKHOLM, ÅBO, HANGÖ, HELSINGFORS	44.50
To HAMBURG, BREMEN, ANTWERP, AMSTERDAM, ROTTERDAM, HAVRE, CHERBOURG	45.00

TURIN, $48.   NAPLES, $52.50.   PIRAEUS, $55.   BEYROUTH, $61., Etc., Etc.

DO NOT DELAY: Secure your tickets through the local Agents or direct from
WHITE STAR LINE, 9 Broadway, New York

TICKETS FOR SALE HERE

Introduction

★

BY BRUCE BEVERIDGE

WHITE STAR LINE'S VISION

THE LATE 19TH AND EARLY 20TH centuries were ambitious times for the steamship industry. Leading the race, or at least tying first, was the British company the White Star Line. Its primary rival was Cunard, another British outfit, which it would merge with in 1935. Cunard and White Star held a government contract to transport mail between the United States and Britain, letting their ships carry the RMS (Royal Mail Steamer) designation.

In 1870, Ismay, Imrie & Co., a shipping company headed by Thomas Ismay, decided the time had arrived for a superior class of screw steamships to run between Liverpool and New York. To accomplish this, they turned to Harland & Wolff, an Irish shipbuilding firm based in Belfast. Harland & Wolff was also a new enterprise, headed by Edward Harland, a creative and enterprising naval architect. Together, Ismay and Harland were destined to change the shipping industry forever.

In 1907, J. Bruce Ismay, son of the late Thomas Ismay and by then chairman of the White Star Line, attended a dinner at the home of Lord William Pirrie, Harland & Wolff's chairman and managing director. It was at this dinner that plans were made for the construction of three huge liners that would be White Star's response to Cunard's new greyhounds, the *Mauretania* and *Lusitania*. Later to be known as the *Olympic*, *Titanic* and *Britannic*, these ships would not compete with the Cunarders in terms of speed, but they would be fast enough to offer a weekly service in each direction between England and North America while providing unparalleled comfort and luxury. The *Olympic* and *Titanic* would be built first, with the *Britannic* to come some time later.

On 31st March 1909, the keel of the *Titanic* was laid at Harland & Wolff, in a berth next to where the *Olympic*'s keel had been laid a few months earlier. On 31st May 1911, the *Titanic* was launched and moved to the fitting-out wharf.

OPPOSITE
The Titanic *during construction at Harland & Wolff's Belfast shipyard.*

BELOW
Marvelling at the ship's propellers.

THE RACE TO BE THE BEST

Cunard's *Mauretania* and *Lusitania* entered commercial service in 1907. Driven entirely by turbine engines, each had a designed speed of over 24 knots, a length of 785 feet and a tonnage of approximately 33,000. They were the largest passenger vessels the world had seen to date – but not for long. As soon as one company launched the newest, largest and fastest ship in the world, another company would design one that was even larger and faster in order to stay ahead of the competition.

ABOVE
*The reception room
outside the* Titanic's
*first-class restaurant,
with wicker furniture
arranged on an
Axminster carpet.*

A SHIP TO RIVAL ALL OTHERS

The *Titanic* was fitted with public rooms and staterooms, decorated in period styles as seen in the best hotels in Europe. It was effectively a floating hotel whose guests were unable to leave. First-class passengers enjoyed a swimming pool, Turkish bath, squash court and a gym, complete with instructor. The first-class public rooms included a dining saloon, reception room, à la carte restaurant, lounge, reading and writing room, smoking room, the Verandah Café and Palm Court. The first-class Grand Staircase extended over 60 feet, from the lower landing to a domed glass skylight above. Decorated in the William and Mary style with carved solid oak panelling, it was the centrepiece of the ship.

Second-class passenger accommodations were as good as first-class on some of the older ships. They too enjoyed a dining room, smoking room and lounge. Third-class passengers had ample promenade space, as well as a large dining saloon with individual seats, instead of the old bench seats of years past. They had a General Room as well as up-to-date toilet facilities.

The *Titanic's* great hull was divided into 16 watertight compartments. This arrangement let her withstand a breach of two adjacent compartments amidships. Furthermore, she was capable of remaining afloat with all of the forward four compartments flooded, a feature intended to protect her if she rammed a floating body in her path. In the view of shipbuilding experts at the time, this made the ship a lifeboat

OPPOSITE
*Advertisements praised
the sheer size of the
*Titanic *and her sister
ship, the* Olympic.

in itself and negated the need for lifeboats to accommodate all on board. More lifeboats were also considered impractical from the standpoint of the deck space required to store them and the number of deckhands needed to crew them.

Accordingly, the completed *Titanic* was fitted with only 20 standard lifeboats. Fourteen of these were 30-foot wooden vessels, permanently suspended beneath double-acting Welin davits. The foremost two were smaller 'emergency cutters', kept permanently swung out at sea in preparation for a swift rescue if someone fell overboard. Two Engelhardt lifeboats, designated C and D, were secured to the deck beneath the emergency cutters. These were termed 'collapsibles' because they had adjustable canvas sides that could be pulled up and braced taut. Two further Engelhardt collapsibles, designated A and B, were secured to the roof of the officers' quarters forward.

The overall length of the *Titanic* was 882 feet 9 inches; the extreme breadth 92 feet 6 inches. From the ship's keel to navigating bridge, the height was 104 feet. There was accommodation for 730 first-class, 560 second-class and 1,200 third-class passengers. When she was completed, the *Titanic* was registered as a British steamship at the port of Liverpool and listed with a gross registered tonnage of 46,383.

On 2nd April 1912, following three years of construction, the *Titanic* weighed anchor and left Belfast Lough for the 570-mile trip from Belfast to Southampton. With the assistance of tugs, she was brought into the River Test. It was just after midnight on 3rd April when the ship was secured near White Star's Berth 44.

LIFEBOAT PROVISION ON THE *TITANIC*

The double-acting Welin davits on the *Titanic* were each capable of launching three or four lifeboats. This was because the ship was originally designed by Harland & Wolff's Alexander Carlisle to carry 64 lifeboats. The number was then decreased to 32. Sometime between 9th and 16th March 1910, the number was further reduced to 16 – the minimum number required by the Board of Trade. By fitting the extra four Engelhardt collapsibles, the White Star Line actually exceeded the Board of Trade requirements by 17 percent for vessels over 10,000 tons.

OLYMPIC AND TITANIC
EACH 45,000 TONS

WHITE STAR LINE

OUT TO SEA

On the morning of Thursday, 4th April, Southampton awoke to find the *Titanic* dressed in flags, a custom in the maritime community to signify a new ship's first day in her port city. Provisioning and crewing commenced in preparation for sailing day. Meanwhile, finishing touches were undertaken to some of her staterooms, including painting fittings and the laying of carpets.

While at Southampton, the ship's deck department saw a reshuffling of the command structure. Captain Smith had just come from the *Olympic* and brought along his Chief Officer, Henry Wilde. This action bounced William Murdoch, who was to have been Chief Officer, to First Officer. This, in turn, moved Charles Lightoller from First to Second Officer and caused the removal of David Blair, the Second Officer who had been aboard for the Belfast-to-Southampton trip. Blair would later send a postcard to his sister expressing his regret at missing the voyage. The junior officers remained as originally assigned, with Herbert Pitman as Third Officer, Joseph Boxhall as Fourth, Harold Lowe as Fifth and James Moody as Sixth.

Also sailing on *Titanic*'s maiden voyage would be Thomas Andrews, as Harland & Wolff's official representative on board. Andrews would rarely be at rest during the voyage, visiting various departments and making copious notes on additions and changes to the ship that would further refine the newest of the White Star fleet.

RIGHT
The ship's officers. Standing, left to right: Herbert McElroy, Chief Purser; Charles Lightoller, Second Officer; Herbert Pitman, Third Officer; Joseph Boxhall, Fourth Officer; Harold Lowe, Fifth Offficer. Seated, left to right: James Moody, Sixth Officer; Henry Wilde, Chief Officer; Captain E. J. Smith; William Murdoch, First Officer.

Sailing day arrived on Wednesday, 10th April. The third-class passengers began to board the ship from about 9.30am. First- and second-class passengers began boarding about an hour before sailing time, as was customary. Many of the more prominent first-class passengers arrived dockside at about 11.30am aboard the South Western Railway 'boat train' from London's Waterloo station. Guests of passengers were allowed aboard for a short period before sailing time, and were informed by a whistle blast when it was time for them to leave.

ABOVE
Thomas Andrews, managing director of Harland & Wolff, was in overall charge of the Titanic's design.

Shortly after noon on 10th April, the *Titanic* departed. Guided by six tugs, she was slowly pulled out of her berth. After the tugs let go of their lines, she was finally alone, under her own power. However, while passing pier 38, where the idle *Oceanic* and the American Line's *New York* were tied, the suction of *Titanic*'s passing caused the *New York* to strain against her mooring lines. One by one, her stern lines parted with sounds like gunshots, snapped, and then her stern began to swing toward the passing liner. The quick-thinking captain of the *Vulcan*, a nearby tug, got a line aboard the *New York* in an attempt to stop her, but to no avail. The *Titanic*'s Captain Smith then undertook a reversing manoeuvre with the reciprocating engine, causing a wake that helped check the American ship. The danger quickly passed and the *Titanic* resumed onwards.

The *Titanic* headed out of Southampton Water and would make two further stops – Cherbourg in France and then Queenstown in Ireland – to collect and drop off passengers, baggage and mail, before steaming out to sea, carrying 1,322 passengers and 885 crew members.

★

INTO THE ICEFIELDS

From noon on Thursday to noon on Friday, the *Titanic* covered 386 miles. Friday to Saturday saw 519 miles made good, and Saturday to Sunday 546 miles. She followed the 'Outward Southern Track' from Queenstown to New York, the route normally followed at this time of year by large steamers. At noon on 14th April, a wireless message was received from the *Baltic*, which warned of field ice. At about 7pm, a second ice warning was received, this time from the *Californian*, which reported ice about 19 miles northward of the track on which the *Titanic* was steaming. Later, there was a third message from the ship *Amerika*, reporting two large icebergs. A fourth message, again sent by the *Californian*, reached the *Titanic* at about 10.40pm on 14th April. It said, 'We are stopped and surrounded by ice.'

On the night of 14th April 1912, the air temperature dropped below freezing. The night sky was moonless. The water was flatter and calmer than many ever remembered. The *Titanic* was steaming at 22½ knots. Despite the warnings of ice, Captain Smith did not reduce speed: it was not felt necessary. Standard practice for the transatlantic mail boats was to hold course and speed, trusting to the crew's ability to see far enough ahead to avoid danger.

At 10pm, Murdoch relieved Second Officer Lightoller on the bridge, reminding him that the ship was within the region where ice had been reported. He also told him of a message he had sent to the crow's nest, reminding the lookouts to exercise extra vigilance in watching for ice. At approximately 11.40pm, lookout Frederick Fleet and his partner Reginald Lee noticed something in the distance appearing out of the darkness. Fleet rang the crow's nest bell three times, the signal for something ahead, and picked up the telephone to the bridge located behind him. The phone was answered by Sixth Officer Moody. A brief exchange took place:

'What did you see?' asked Moody.
'Iceberg right ahead,' replied Fleet.
'Thank you,' acknowledged Moody.

BELOW
Frederick Fleet, one of the two ship's lookouts on the night of Sunday, 14th April.

Murdoch, who had also seen the berg, ordered 'hard-a-starboard' in order to swing the ship's head to port, and telegraphed 'stop' down to the engine room for both engines and 'full astern'. When the *Titanic* struck the iceberg an estimated 37 seconds after the lookouts' initial sighting, the quartermaster at the wheel had got the helm 'hard over' and the ship turned about 22½ degrees to port. The initial impact occurred below the waterline on her starboard bow. Murdoch immediately rang the alarm bell and pulled the lever that closed the automatic watertight doors below. As the iceberg passed the bridge, Captain Smith entered from his quarters near the wheelhouse and asked what they had struck. Murdoch was reported to have replied, 'An iceberg, sir. I hard-a-starboarded and reversed the engines, and I was going to hard-a-port round it, but she was too close. I could not do any more.' Smith gave the order for the carpenter to sound the ship and to 'get all the boats out and serve out the belts'.

ABOVE
A cross section showing the compartments that would flood soon after the collision.

As the ship's hull scraped along the iceberg, the unyielding mass of ice caused the shell plates to intermittently buckle and separate. The *Titanic* had been fatally damaged along a 300-foot stretch of her hull, 10 feet above the keel. Although the total area open to the sea was no more than 12 square feet, the tremendous water pressure at depth forced water in at a rate that caused the flooding compartments to fill rapidly. As the water rose in the five flooded compartments, the ship began to settle by the bows. It would only be a matter of time before water rose above the after bulkhead of the fifth watertight compartment and began flooding the sixth. The *Titanic* was going to founder.

'COME QUICKLY, DISTRESS'

As soon as the extent of the flooding became known, Captain Smith directed the Marconi operators to send out a distress call. The first 'CQD' went out at 12.15am local ship's time.

The *Titanic*'s distress call was heard by a number of other ships and the shore station at Cape Race, Newfoundland. As far as they could tell, the nearest ship was 58 miles away: the 13,600-ton Cunard steamship *Carpathia*, bound to the Mediterranean from New York. By pure luck or chance, her wireless operator Harold Cottam, who had gone off duty, had switched his set back on just to listen. Cottam answered the *Titanic*'s call for help. The *Carpathia*'s captain, Arthur Rostron, immediately ordered full speed and issued a series of orders to wake all off-duty crew and make preparations to receive survivors. With her top speed normally being 14½ knots, Rostron did not think they could be there for another four hours.

ABOVE
A distress call sent to the Russian steamer SS Birma at 1.40am.

Immediately following the collision, all of the *Titanic*'s deckhands were called and told to 'clear the boats' – uncover the lifeboats and make them ready. At 12.20am, the order was given to swing them out and lower them to the edge of the deck for loading. Under the supervision of the Chief Officer, two senior officers and three junior officers, this order was duly followed, and women and children were asked to begin boarding. There was complete calm. Staying on the ship, which had not yet taken on any appreciable list, seemed far safer than boarding a seemingly frail lifeboat and descending to the dark, vast ocean.

Down below, the bedroom stewards were attempting to rouse their passengers and send them up on deck. Many did not want to leave the warmth of the cabins or lounges for the freezing air of the boat deck when the ship was not obviously in peril. The lack of any urgency or general announcements, combined with the strains of orchestra music, made any talk of boarding lifeboats seem surreal.

OPPOSITE
A sketch of the sinking by passenger John Thayer.

While the loading of lifeboats was commencing, Fourth Officer Boxhall began sending up distress rockets. Eight rockets were fired over a period of an hour. Yet they did not attract help from what appeared to be a ship some 5 or 8 miles away, nor did it respond to signals sent from one of the ship's Morse lamps.

By 1.55am, all of the lifeboats except for the two collapsibles on the roof of the officers' quarters deckhouse had left the ship. Those who were now safely off the ship lay off at various distances. Some had attempted to pull for the lights of the steamer that appeared nearby. As the *Titanic* continued to go down by the head, her stern began to rise out of the water. Shortly before her final moments, the ship's lights flickered and dimmed, then went out. During her final, foundering moments, the *Titanic*'s great hull broke in two. Her stern section briefly settled back into the water before rising into the air, straightening out into a position perpendicular to the water, and descending into the depths like an elevator.

THE ABANDONED THIRD CLASS

Third-class passengers faced a different set of obstacles, not least of which was that many could not speak English. Contrary to often-repeated stories, there were no locked gates. Any physical barriers between third-class and other areas of the ship were in place only to mark the boundaries, and could be opened by anyone. However, many of these passengers simply waited obediently for someone to tell them what to do, and no one did. Most who did eventually make it to the boat deck found the lifeboats had already gone.

THE SAVED, AND THE LOST

The saved can be classified as follows:

First-class: 201 out of 324

Second-class: 118 out of 277

Third-class: 181 out of 708

Officers & crew: 211 out of 885

(Figure includes 22 stewardesses saved)

Postmen & musicians: 1 out of 13

Had the *Titanic* been supplied with lifeboats for all on board, many more would have been saved.

TOO LATE

At 2.35am, with nothing heard from the *Titanic* for the past half hour, the *Carpathia* transmitted, 'If you are there, we are firing rockets.' Captain Rostron had ordered the continuous firing of pyrotechnic signals to give hope to the *Titanic*'s passengers and crew. It was a harrowing time, as Rostron later reported: 'Icebergs loomed up and fell astern and we never slackened. It was an anxious time with the *Titanic*'s fateful experience very close in our minds. There were 700 souls on *Carpathia* and those lives as well as the survivors of the *Titanic* herself depended on the sudden turn of the wheel.'

At 4am, the *Carpathia* reached the *Titanic*'s reported position. Shortly thereafter, Rostron sighted Lifeboat 2. The other lifeboats were scattered over an area of 4 to 5 square miles. The *Carpathia* picked up all of the lifeboats' passengers and, with the exception of one 30-foot lifeboat and one collapsible that were considered too damaged to salvage, hauled up the boats. Rostron then set course back to New York with 712 survivors, one of whom died shortly afterwards.

At 2.20am on 15th April 1912, 1,495 lives were lost in the sinking of the White Star Liner *Titanic*. Her watertight bulkheads, which had earned her the strapline 'practically unsinkable', served only to delay her sinking. The latest, the largest and supposedly the safest of ocean liners sank to the bottom of the ocean in less than three hours.

The collision was the result of daring navigation, but the loss of life was due to the lack of lifeboats and the failure to fill completely the few that were available. The *Titanic*'s speed on that fatal night was between 21 and 23 knots, although the ship's officers knew icebergs were near. The size of the ship and her safety features gave them a false sense of security. In spite of warnings that there was a large field of ice ahead, the captain followed the usual practice of the time: if the ship runs at full speed into the zone of danger, she will brush the ice floes aside; providing the night is clear, anything large enough to cause damage will be sighted in enough time to be avoided.

The wreck of the *Titanic* left the shipping world a number of issues to address, but overwhelmingly of these was the necessity of safeguarding life at sea. Following the disaster, two official investigations, one conducted by a committee of the United States Senate and the other by a British commission under the auspices of the Board of Trade, worked to elicit facts and to draw conclusions. As the details came out in personal testimonies before these two bodies, and from the accounts of survivors, public feeling wavered between surging pride at the way in which death was confronted by most of those on the *Titanic*, and surging indignation, as the conviction grew that the loss of life was a needless sacrifice that could easily have been averted.

After the *Titanic*'s demise, the shipping industry was required to provide sufficient lifeboats on its ocean-going steamers for all passengers. Ships with wireless telegraphy had to be manned around the clock, and the operators used SOS as the standard distress call.

An international ice patrol was created to monitor iceberg movements in the North Atlantic. If the tragedy of the *Titanic* can be said to have had any positive outcome, it was that it awakened a world that had become complacent and too trusting of man's technology.

BELOW
*J. Bruce Ismay, President
of the White Star Line,
is questioned at the
US Senate Inquiry.*

JOHN JACOB & MADELEINE ASTOR

DICKINSON & HELEN BISHOP

ALBERT & VERA DICK

HENRY & CLARA FRAUENTHAL

GEORGE & DOROTHY HARDER

DANIEL & MARY MARVIN

VICTOR & PEPITA PEÑASCO

The Honeymooners

★

LUCIAN & ELOISE SMITH

JOHN & NELLE SNYDER

EDWARD & ETHEL BEANE

JOHN & LIZZIE CHAPMAN

JOHN & KATE BOURKE

NEAL & EILEEN McNAMEE

PASSENGER MANIFEST

1ST

CLASS

Name, ... *John Jacob Astor (b. 13th July 1864).*

Name, ... *Madeleine Talmage Force (b. 19th June 1893).*

Married, ... *9th September 1911.*

Point of embarkation, ... *Cherbourg.*

Ticket no. ...... *17757.* Suite, ... *C62/4.*

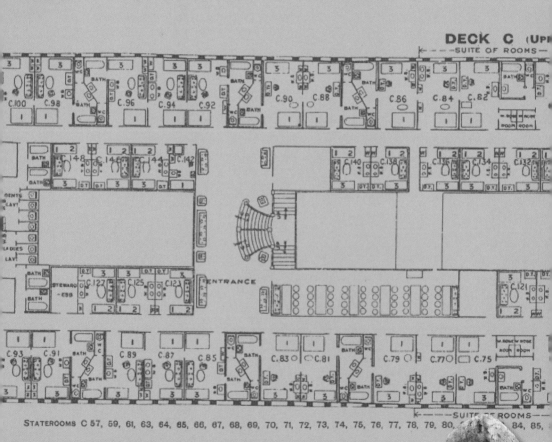

DECK C (UPP
— SUITE OF ROOMS —

STATEROOMS C 57, 59, 61, 63, 64, 65, 66, 67, 68, 69, 70, 71, 72, 73, 74, 75, 76, 77, 78, 79, 80, 84, 85,

— SUITE OF ROOMS —

John Jacob & Madeleine Astor

It's hard to credit the scandal it caused when John Jacob Astor divorced his first wife, Ava, in 1909, and then two years later announced that he was remarrying. His actions weren't unprecedented – others had divorced and remarried in that era – but John Jacob was an Astor, the next best thing the United States had to royalty. There were some in upper-class society who would never forgive him.

I T HAD LONG BEEN WHISPERED THAT the Astors' marriage was an unhappy one. It was a poorly kept secret that Ava had a lover, and the rumour spread that her daughter, Ava Muriel, was not John's child. The divorce proceedings were hostile, and Ava finally walked away with a settlement that was much less than she had hoped for. John got custody of their son, Vincent, while Ava Muriel stayed with her mother.

This would have been just about acceptable to society, but then it was rumoured that John was wooing a debutante called Madeleine Talmage Force, a girl who was a year younger than his son. They had been introduced in August 1910 when Madeleine was fresh from completing her course at Miss Spence's prestigious finishing school in New York and was vacationing in Bar Harbor, Maine. Madeleine was bowled over when John Astor showed an interest. Handsome, erudite, considerate and charming, he was by far the nicest, most fascinating man she had met. He charmed her with flowers and books that he thought she might like, and she quickly fell in love.

ABOVE
Madeleine was just eighteen years old on her honeymoon.

He charmed her with flowers and books that he thought she might like, and she quickly fell in love.

John and his new sweetheart were seen together at the opera, where Madeleine sat in the Astors' private box, at the Poughkeepsie boat race and out dining in fashionable restaurants, and every sighting was reported and scrutinized by the media. Their engagement was eventually announced in August 1911, when he was forty-seven years old and she was just eighteen. They wanted to marry as soon as possible, but there was a problem: John couldn't find a minister who would agree to marry them in a religious ceremony. Despite the offer of a generous fee, several turned him down.

OPPOSITE
Madeleine and John Jacob Astor with their Airedale, Kitty.

THE WEALTH OF THE ASTORS

The Astor family arrived in the United States in the 18th century and amassed its fortune in the fur trade. Great-grandson of those original settlers, John Jacob Astor IV inherited acres of land and property in Manhattan worth a total of $100 million ($37 billion in today's terms), making him one of the wealthiest men in the world. John Jacob increased the family's holdings by building the Astoria Hotel in Park Avenue to adjoin the Waldorf owned by his cousin William, thereby creating a complex that came to be known as 'the world's most luxurious hotel'.

Not content with managing the family business, John found time to invent several mechanical devices, including a bicycle brake, a turbine engine and a machine that could produce gas from peat moss. He also wrote a bizarre science-fiction novel about life in the year 2000 on the planets Saturn and Jupiter, and served as a colonel in the 1898 Spanish–American war.

Finally, the Reverend Joseph Lambert agreed to officiate, and the wedding took place at Beechwood, the Astors' luxurious Rhode Island home, on 9th September 1911. Witnesses said it was a very romantic occasion. John was clearly madly in love, and leaped forward to grab Madeleine's hand as soon as she appeared on her father's arm. After the ceremony, however, the Reverend Lambert was so vilified by other members of the New York clergy that he resigned from the ministry in disgust.

OPPOSITE
The Astors' Fifth Avenue home, which overlooked Central Park.

THE HONEYMOON

Both shocked by the vitriolic coverage of their union in the American press, John and Madeleine decided to take an extended honeymoon, in the hope that the frenzy would have subsided on their return. On 24th January 1912, they sailed to Europe on board the *Olympic*, sister ship to the *Titanic*, which was still being fitted out in Belfast's Harland & Wolff ship-yard. Accompanying them were John's valet, Victor Robbins, Madeleine's maid, Rosalie Bidois, and their pet Airedale, Kitty. They also took a nurse, Caroline Endres, because Madeleine was three months pregnant when they sailed. Although the mother-to-be was healthy, they didn't want to take any risks.

Among John and Madeleine's fellow passengers on board the *Olympic* was a gregarious woman called Maggie Brown, who had already forged a reputation as a formidable campaigner for woman's suffrage. She joined the Astors in Cairo, where they viewed the pyramids together, and she even helped to find Kitty one day when she ran off. Maggie accompanied the Astors to Italy and then to Paris, but when

BELOW
The couple were photo-graphed by the press whenever they went out.

THE *TITANIC*'S SISTER SHIP CRASHES

The *Olympic*'s maiden voyage launched in June 1911, making her still a brand-new ship when the Astors boarded her for their outward-bound trip to Europe. However, she had already been involved in a collision. On 20th September 1911, the *Olympic* ran into a British Navy ship, HMS *Hawke*. The resulting hole in her side caused two of her bulkhead compartments to flood and twisted the propeller shaft. She had to limp back to Belfast for expensive repairs, and this slowed work on the *Titanic*, whose maiden voyage was put back from 20th March to 10th April. At a subsequent inquiry, Captain Edward Smith was criticized for sailing too close to HMS *Hawke*, but this didn't stop the White Star Line from putting him in charge of the *Titanic* when she finally made it out of the shipyard. Stewardess Violet Jessop would have the distinction of surviving both the *Olympic*'s collision and the sinking of the *Titanic*.

she got word that her grandson was ill back home, she decided to book a transatlantic passage on the *Titanic*, boarding at Cherbourg.

'Can we go too?' Madeleine had asked John. 'I don't want to risk the baby being born overseas.'

Her doting husband agreed, and booked their ticket to sail on 10th April. The *Titanic* was too big to dock at Cherbourg harbour, so they were ferried out to her on a tender. On boarding, they were assigned a superior suite of rooms, C62/4, one of the best on the ship.

Madeleine was impressed by the luxury of the great ship, but shocked and hurt by the behaviour of the other first-class passengers, who ostracized them, turning away as they entered the dining room and refusing to sit near them. John's first wife Ava was renowned for her beauty and elegance, and many of her friends were on board. It was hard for Madeleine, a plain girl still in her teens, to step into those shoes, and she later complained to friends that she had overheard women whispering to each other, mocking her dress and hairstyle and making very unflattering comparisons with her predecessor. She might have taken to eating her meals in her cabin were it not for the warm friendship of Maggie Brown, who scoffed at the gossips on board and encouraged her to simply ignore them.

On the night of Sunday, 14th April, the Astors ate dinner with Maggie, then retired to their suite for an early night.

THE NIGHT OF 14TH APRIL

John Jacob Astor had felt the *Titanic* hitting something at 11.40pm and went on deck to investigate. When he returned to their suite, he told his wife that the ship had struck ice but that the damage did not appear to be serious. Shortly after midnight, however, there was a knock on the door and they

OPPOSITE
The first-class dining room, with Jacobean-style decor.

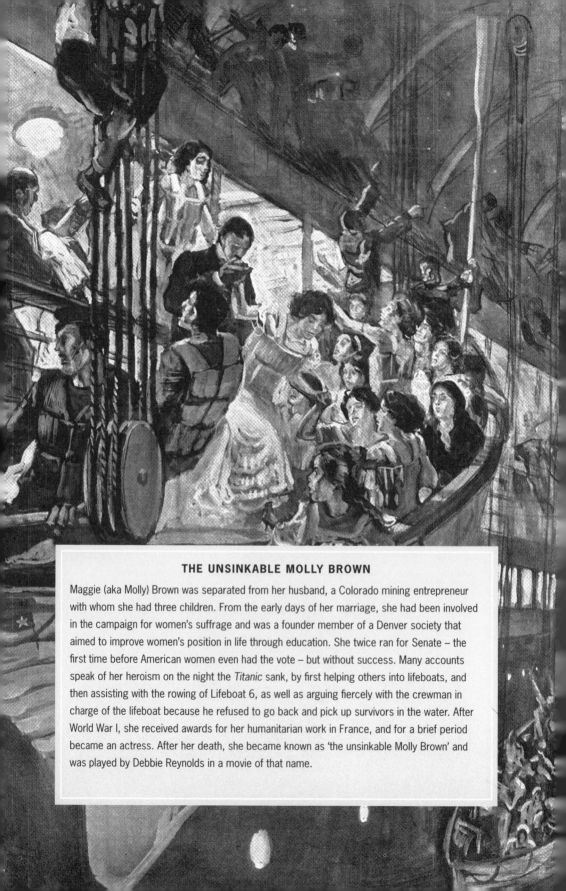

THE UNSINKABLE MOLLY BROWN

Maggie (aka Molly) Brown was separated from her husband, a Colorado mining entrepreneur with whom she had three children. From the early days of her marriage, she had been involved in the campaign for women's suffrage and was a founder member of a Denver society that aimed to improve women's position in life through education. She twice ran for Senate – the first time before American women even had the vote – but without success. Many accounts speak of her heroism on the night the *Titanic* sank, by first helping others into lifeboats, and then assisting with the rowing of Lifeboat 6, as well as arguing fiercely with the crewman in charge of the lifeboat because he refused to go back and pick up survivors in the water. After World War I, she received awards for her humanitarian work in France, and for a brief period became an actress. After her death, she became known as 'the unsinkable Molly Brown' and was played by Debbie Reynolds in a movie of that name.

were told by a steward that the captain wanted them on deck in their life-jackets.

OPPOSITE
Women were helped into Lifeboat 4 from a covered promenade.

'It will only be a precaution,' John soothed Madeleine. 'Nothing to worry about.'

The pair made their way to the boat deck, where several other couples were standing around awaiting instructions. Now that the ship had come to a halt, her engines were letting off steam and it was so noisy they could barely hear each other speak. John saw Captain Smith descending the steps from the bridge and went to have a word with him. Less influential passengers might not have gained the captain's ear so readily. The captain told John that the collision had been serious, and that women and children were to be loaded into the lifeboats.

'Don't tell anyone else,' the captain cautioned. 'I don't want to spread panic.'

John took Madeleine into the gymnasium. They sat on a mechanical horse and he explained to her that she would have to get into a boat.

'Can't I stay here with you?' she pleaded.

John had to say no. 'The captain has said that the men must get on boats later. That's the way it is.'

Madeleine was by now severely alarmed. John used his penknife to split open his own life-jacket, showing her the cork inside that would make it buoyant. 'Not that any of us is going in the water, of course,' he added quickly.

At 12.45am, Second Officer Lightoller lowered Lifeboat 4, intending to let passengers board from the closed-in promenade on A Deck. When he discovered the promenade's windows were closed, he turned his attention to other boats while a steward went down to open them. John Astor had been hoping that help would arrive before it was necessary for them to get into the boats, but this didn't happen. By the time Lifeboat 4 was being loaded, at 1.40am, the *Titanic* had a severe list.

'It's time to go now, darling,' he said.

Despite Madeleine's protests, John helped her over the 4-foot rail and down into the boat. 'Might I join my wife?' he asked Lightoller. 'She's in a delicate condition.'

'No, sir,' was the reply. 'No men are allowed in the boats until all the women have been loaded.'

John took the refusal bravely. He helped Rosalie Bidois and Caroline Endres to board, then he waved and called good-bye to Madeleine as the lifeboat was lowered to the black, still water down below.

As they rowed off, Madeleine looked back and thought she could see Kitty, their dog, running around on the deck. 'John must have gone to get her,' she thought. 'I do hope she will be rescued as well.'

At that stage, Madeleine didn't know about the shortage of lifeboats. She had no idea that the ship was going to sink. She watched with horror as it slipped lower and lower into the dark waters, upended and finally disappeared into the deep. She listened, distraught, to the people in the water crying for help and prayed that John was on another of the lifeboats that they could see bobbing about around them.

Their boat picked up eight survivors from the water. Two of them died on board.

THE DYING MOMENTS

There are various unsubstantiated rumours about John's bravery in the final half-hour before the ship sank. Some say he made his way to the kennels and set free all the dogs; others that he helped to disguise a young boy as a woman so he could get a place on one of the last lifeboats; yet more witnesses say that he helped some women to board these last boats, guiding them through the crowds to safety. When the ship went down, he was seen standing near the great funnel. A piece of debris may have knocked him unconscious because he doesn't appear to have made an attempt to swim to any of the boats, although he must have been quite close to some of them.

Madeleine helped with the rowing on Lifeboat 4, despite her delicate condition. As dawn broke, they saw the huge shape of the *Carpathia* on the horizon and headed toward her, reaching her side at 6am. When she was pulled aboard, Madeleine asked repeatedly if anyone had seen her husband, but no one had. She was taken to the ship's infirmary for a check-up then given a room to herself, in which she sat and wept. Rosalie Bidois and Caroline Endres tried to comfort her by suggesting that he might be on another ship, or could have climbed onto an iceberg and be waiting to be picked up. But to no avail.

When the news of the tragedy broke in New York on Monday 15th, John's son, Vincent Astor, rushed straight to the White Star office. He was seen leaving a little later in tears, having heard the news that the *Titanic* had sunk. Next, he rushed to the offices of Marconi, the wireless operators, but they did not have a list of survivors. He hurried on to Associated Press and scanned their latest reports.

DEATH BEFORE DISHONOUR

Second Officer Lightoller adhered strictly to the rule 'women and children first', even when it meant sending some boats off less than half full because he couldn't persuade any more women to board them. On the starboard side of the ship, the rule wasn't taken so literally; when there were spaces on a boat and no more women around, the crew members let men get on. It is surprising that the richest, most famous man on the *Titanic* was unable to get a place on a lifeboat. He may have been successful if he had used bribery – he had around $2,500 in his pocket – but that would not have been an option for him. John Jacob Astor had been brought up to honour his family name and act like a gentleman.

THE *MACKAY-BENNETT*

The grisly task of collecting bodies from the waters of the North Atlantic fell to the crew of a Halifax ship called the *Mackay-Bennett*. As they pulled each body on board, the crewmen took detailed notes of physical characteristics, pocket contents, jewellery and clothing. By 27th April, they had recovered 306 bodies, including that of John Jacob Astor, who was identified by the 'J. J. A.' embroidered on his collar; by his gold pocket watch, which had stopped at 3.20am, an hour after the *Titanic* went down; by a platinum ring studded with diamonds; and by a gold belt buckle that had been in the family for generations. The crew of the *Mackay-Bennett* gave sea burials to the bodies that were badly damaged or decomposed, and the rest were taken back to Halifax for burial. Vincent Astor sent the family train to pick up his father's body, and a private funeral was held near the family's Rhode Island estate.

It was later that day, when the first list of survivors was wired from the *Carpathia*, that Vincent learned that his new stepmother was on board but that his father was not. He broke down and sobbed, telling the wire operator that he would give him all his fortune if he could just offer news of his father's safety. The operator could, of course, do no such thing.

Such was the importance of the Astors in the United States that many of the next day's papers led with the news that John Jacob Astor had been killed, reporting almost as an afterthought that some 1,500 other souls were also missing. A reporter for the *Evening Telegram* commented that the stock exchange was unlikely to be affected because the bulk of Astor's fortune was in real estate.

Vincent Astor tried to arrange for the family yacht to collect Madeleine from the *Carpathia*, but was talked out of it by White Star officials. Instead, he met Madeleine when the ship docked at New York, and had to break the news to her that there were no more boats and that her new husband could not possibly still be alive.

THE NEXT GENERATION

Exactly four months after the sinking of the *Titanic*, on 14th August 1912, Madeleine gave birth to a baby boy, whom she called John Jacob, after his father. Under the terms of a prenuptial arrangement designed to protect the Astor holdings, she was entitled to interest on a trust fund of $5 million for as long as she did not remarry. This was plenty for a young woman to live on, but it doesn't appear to have been important to Madeleine. She just wanted her husband back.

She remained in mourning for a long time, keeping herself locked away at home with her

> *For Madeleine, it had never been about the money; she had married John Jacob Astor for love.*

baby and seeing only a few very close friends and family members. However, she was still young, and resilient. In June 1916, she married childhood friend William Dick and thus relinquished her rights to the Astor money. She went on to have two more sons with him. Dick was a banker, not a multi-millionaire, but he was able to provide for her in more or less the style to which she was accustomed.

When she married John Jacob Astor, the gossips had accused Madeleine of being after his money and social standing. Why else, they argued, would a young girl choose a husband almost thirty years her senior? However, the overwhelming weight of the evidence belies this. It seems that for John and Madeleine, it was only ever about love.

ABOVE
John Jacob Astor IV was buried in Trinity Church Cemetery, New York. Although the funeral service was kept private, scores of people turned out to watch the funeral procession.

PASSENGER MANIFEST

1ST CLASS

Name, *Dickinson Bishop (b. 24th March 1887).*

Name, *Helen Walton (b. 19th May 1892).*

Married, *November 1911.*

Point of embarkation, *Cherbourg.*

Ticket no. *11967.* **Suite,** *B49.*

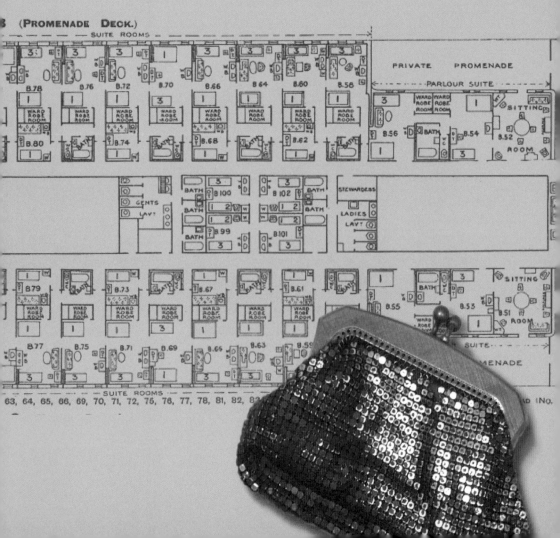

Dickinson & Helen Bishop

Mr. and Mrs. D. H. Bishop

While visiting Egypt as part of her four-month honeymoon, Helen Bishop was told by a fortune-teller that she would survive a shipwreck and then an earthquake, but meet her death in a car accident. Floating in Lifeboat 7, after the sinking of the *Titanic*, she related that story to give hope to her fellow passengers. She can't have realized how uncannily close to the truth the prophecy would prove to be.

THIS PAGE
Trips to exotic destinations, such as Paris and Venice, were options available to only the wealthiest of people.

1102. The Rialto and Grand Canal, Venice, Italy,
Copyright 1902, by C. L. Wasson

AT THE AGE OF TWENTY-THREE, Dickinson Bishop became a wealthy widower when his first wife died, leaving him a major share in the Round Oak Stove Company. This family business was renowned for its efficient wood-burning stoves, and was the main employer in the small town of Dowagiac in south-west Michigan.

Nineteen-year-old Helen Walton was a stunning, dark-haired girl from nearby Sturgis, whose father owned the Royal Easy Chair Company, notable for producing a chair that reclined at the press of a button in its arm. When Helen was introduced to Dick Bishop, she was immediately drawn to him. He was still wearing a black armband in mourning for his first wife, and she felt strong compassion for him. As they spent more and more time together, that compassion quickly turned to love. They were married in November 1911, and embarked on a no-expense-spared honeymoon that took them to Algiers, Egypt, Italy and France.

Dickinson doted on his new bride and could deny her nothing, showering her with gifts at every stop along their travels. In Florence, he bought her a little lapdog called Frou-Frou, a yappy little creature that she adored. Shortly afterwards, Helen discovered that she was pregnant, and Dickinson was beside himself with happiness. What could be more perfect?

When they read in the newspapers about the luxurious amenities on board the newly built *Titanic*, Dickinson suggested that they delay their journey home in order to sail on her maiden voyage. It would be a fitting end to their idyllic honeymoon. Helen gladly agreed, and they boarded the ship at Cherbourg on Wednesday, 10th April.

BELOW
A tender brought passengers out to board the Titanic *at Cherbourg because the port was too small to accommodate her.*

ABOVE
A curtained four-poster bed in a first-class stateroom; from the wood panelling to the bed linen, everything was of the very best quality.

THE END OF AN IDYLLIC TRIP

Dick and Helen were a sociable couple and made friends with several other first-class passengers. They weren't part of the snobbish crowd who ostracized the Astors, and Helen formed a quick attachment with Madeleine, who was a year younger than her, also pregnant, and a fellow dog lover. The Bishops also got to know the Harders from New York City, and a man called Albert A. Stewart, who had the suite opposite theirs on B Deck, with whom they chatted in the lounge.

On the evening of 14th April, the Bishops socialized in the public lounge and stopped on deck to watch the sunset, which was particularly stunning that night. They lingered, arms wrapped around each other, as the last rays of sun faded and the sky became studded with stars. It couldn't have been more romantic, although they both noticed the temperature had dropped significantly from the day before.

Their suite had a stateroom where they could sit and relax, and an interconnecting door led into the bedroom and marble-fitted bathroom. When the *Titanic* hit the iceberg at 11.40pm, Helen had already retired to bed and Dick was reading the newspaper next door. Neither of them felt the jolt, but a few minutes later Albert Stewart knocked on their door and told Dick that he thought the boat had struck something.

Dick woke Helen, trying not to alarm her. 'We'd better go up on deck, just to be on the safe side,' he said.

She pulled on some clothes and they went up to A Deck, where they found some other people milling around, including the Astors.

'Darling, I don't suppose you could go and fetch my muff from the room?' Helen asked her husband. Her hands were freezing in the bitter cold.

While Dickinson was away fulfilling this request, John Astor spotted Captain Smith coming down the stairs and went to talk to him. On his return to the party, he had some worrying news.

'The captain says we should all put on life-jackets. It seems we may have to get into the lifeboats while they assess the damage to the ship.'

Helen hurried down to their cabin to tell Dickinson, and they both pulled on their life-jackets. They agreed it was better to be safe than sorry.

'What about Frou-Frou?' Helen asked, clutching her little pet. 'Can I bring her with us?'

'It's only a precaution,' Dickinson assured her. 'Your darling Frou-Frou will still be here when we get back.'

Helen kissed the little dog before placing her on a couch. They left the suite, locking the door behind them.

DOGS ON THE *TITANIC*

There were 12 dogs on board the *Titanic*. The three that survived were smuggled by their owners onto lifeboats and hidden on their laps. There was a Pekingese on Lifeboat 3 and a Pomeranian on both Lifeboats 6 and 7. Helen Bishop must have looked at the Pomeranian on her boat, owned by a woman called Margaret Hays, and bitterly regretted her decision not to bring Frou-Frou. First-class passenger Ann Isham had been travelling with a large dog, variously reported to be a Great Dane or a Saint Bernard, and one theory is that she refused to get on a lifeboat without him. Two days after the sinking of the *Titanic*, passengers on the German liner *Bremen* reported seeing the body of a woman in a life-jacket floating on the surface, her arms wrapped around a large dog. However, there is no firm evidence to back this report, and Ann Isham's body was never recovered.

'It's only a precaution ...
Frou-Frou will still be
here when we get back.'

LIFEBOAT 7

Back on A Deck, the Bishops found a small group waiting on the starboard side of the ship, where a lifeboat was being readied by the crew. It was cranked outward until it hung suspended 75 feet above the dark water. There was no panic, just a general muttering as people wondered what to do.

An officer came up and took Helen by the arm, guiding her toward the boat. 'Be very quiet,' he said, 'and get in the boat immediately.' She was the first passenger on the *Titanic* to board a lifeboat.

Dickinson later claimed that, as he helped his wife over the edge, a hand pushed him from behind and he stumbled forward into the boat, where he sat down on one of the bench seats next to his wife. Further passengers climbed in, and then Dickinson squeezed his wife's shoulders as the boat was lowered slowly down to the icy ocean surface.

Once on the water, the crewmen began to row away from the ship. 'Let's have a head count!' one crewman cried, and the assembled passengers each called out the next number when it was their turn. There were 28 passengers in total. Helen counted 12 women and 13 men, as well as the three crew members. The boat was half empty, with plenty of spare seats, but she didn't give it any thought at that stage, assuming there would be more than sufficient boats for all passengers.

They watched other boats being lowered, and began to talk among themselves. 'Do you really think the *Titanic* is going to sink?' 'Won't the suction pull us under if she does?' 'How long do you think it will be before another ship comes to rescue us?' 'Is one on the way?' The crewmen had no more answers than the passengers.

Helen tried to comfort everyone by relating the Egyptian fortune-teller's prediction. 'We have to be rescued in order for the rest of my prophecy to be true,' she told them.

There was another honeymoon couple on Lifeboat 7, and several unmarried men. The men were asked to help with the rowing and began to take turns at relieving the crew. Helen later remembered a French aviator called Pierre Maréchal, who never once took the monocle from his eye. A German man who claimed to be a baron sat smoking throughout, refusing to help row, even after Helen took a turn herself.

OPPOSITE
Those in lifeboats rowed away quickly in case they were sucked under when the ship sank. In the absence of photographs, newspapers showed dramatic illustrations of the tragedy.

THE TIME LINE

Dickinson Bishop caused some confusion when he testified to the US Senate Inquiry that Lifeboat 7, the first to be launched, was not lowered to the water until around 12.45am on 15th April. If he was correct, the evacuation of passengers had begun over an hour after the collision, which all reports place at 11.40pm on the 14th. The reports of crew members indicate an earlier launch time for Lifeboat 7, of around 12.27am or 12.28am, just minutes before Lifeboat 5, which hit the water at 12.30am. It was 2.20am when the *Titanic* finally sank, and just after 5am when the Bishops boarded the *Carpathia*, after three hours drifting in the North Atlantic. It must have been the longest three hours of their lives.

" The Titanic looked enormous "

Boat Deck
clear of boats

"The bows & bridge
completely under water"

" Sea calm as a pond
There was just a gentle heave"

About fifteen minutes after they left the *Titanic*, another lifeboat drew up alongside them. This boat was fuller, so five passengers clambered across onto Lifeboat 7, causing it to rock alarmingly. Everyone shifted to make room for the newcomers, which included a baby, and they rowed on until they were over a mile from the *Titanic*. The ocean surface was still and glassy, with barely a ripple.

Helen and Dickinson had a clear view of the *Titanic* as it sunk. One set of portholes disappeared beneath the waterline, and then another. Finally, the stern rose up as the ship listed forward. As Helen later described, 'For a moment, the ship seemed to be pointing straight down, looking like a gigantic whale submerging itself, head first.' As it disappeared beneath the water, they heard a wave of 'death cries and groans' as the remaining passengers were flung into the icy North Atlantic.

The crew members on Lifeboat 7 had brought along green flares, which they lit occasionally, but the flashes of light raised false hopes of rescue among the occupants of other lifeboats and the few people still floating on pieces of debris in the water. Everyone on the boat shivered violently as the cold ate into their bones. Helen Bishop took off her woollen stockings and gave them to a young girl who had got dressed in such a hurry that her legs were bare.

BELOW
In shock and exhausted, survivors reach the Carpathia. *Although food and water had been left in the lifeboats, no one found them in the black of night.*

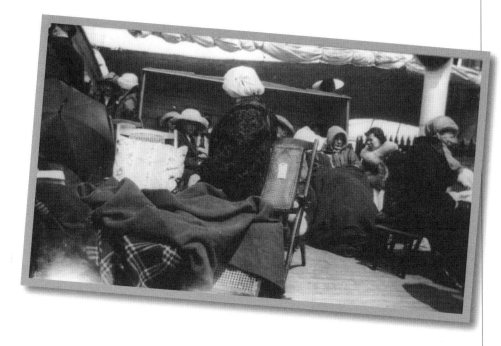

ON BOARD THE *CARPATHIA*

Dawn began to break over the still waters, and the occupants of Lifeboat 7 saw a dark shape appear on the horizon. As soon as they realized that it was a ship, the crewmen began to row hard towards it. For most of the last few hours there had been silence on the boat, with each person lost in his or her own thoughts. Now the mood turned to celebration.

'We're going to be rescued. Oh, thank God!' Helen cried, and Dickinson kissed her.

They pulled alongside the *Carpathia*. Chairs were lowered on ropes for the women to sit in and be lifted up to deck, but Helen insisted she was perfectly capable of climbing the ladder herself. Once on board, every hospitality was offered to them: food, drink, blankets and medical care, if needed. The Bishops began to chat to other passengers and it was only gradually, over the next few hours, that they realized quite how many people had been unable to get a place on a lifeboat and had perished when the ship sank. Their elation on being rescued turned to profound sadness as they spoke to woman after woman who had lost her husband. They heard, too, that John Astor was missing.

ABOVE
Survivors sat huddled in blankets on the Carpathia's *decks.*

SURVIVOR'S MESSAGES FROM THE *CARPATHIA*

Harold Bride, the younger of the *Titanic*'s two wireless operators, was rescued from the water but his feet were badly injured. He was taken to the *Carpathia*'s infirmary and stayed there for ten hours before hearing that the ship's wireless operator, Harold Cottam, was overwhelmed with work, because so many survivors wanted to send messages to let their relatives know that they were alive. He limped on crutches to the wireless room and spent the rest of the trip working there. The two men ignored all requests for information from the press, and even failed to respond to an enquiry from US President William Taft about a friend of his, but by 17th April most survivors' names were known on shore.

Dickinson Bishop sent two wires from the *Carpathia*: one to the manager at the Round Oak Stove Works and the other to his parents, saying simply, 'On board the *Carpathia*, all are well. Signed, Dick.' The messages were received on the morning of Thursday, 18th April, and the *Carpathia* docked in New York City at 8pm that evening.

THE SENATE INQUIRY

Helen and Dickinson had originally planned to get their chauffeur to drive them straight from New York back home to Michigan in their brand new Lozier, the most expensive car available at that time. However, they had lost all their clothing on the *Titanic*, as well as $11,000-worth of Helen's jewellery, so they decided to stay at the Waldorf-Astoria just long enough to replenish their wardrobes. While they were staying in the hotel, they were contacted and asked if they would testify in front of the US Senate Inquiry into the sinking of the *Titanic*, which was due to begin shortly, on 19th April.

They were called on the eleventh day, and Helen was first to testify. She spoke clearly and concisely, relating the sequence of events from the initial collision through to their rescue.

VOL. 16 NO. 66 *April 17 1912* DOWAGIAC, MIC

CARPATHIA LANDS IN NEW YORK CITY AND THE BISHOPS WIRE THEY'RE SAFE

Mrs. Bishop Is First Lady to Leave the Wrecked Ocean Liner

SEND A WIRELESS

First Direct Tidings Came Last Night, and Again This Morning they Send a Message Home

Mr. and Mrs. D. H. Bishop, passengers on the wrecked steamship Titanic, and rescued by the Carpathia hours after the wrecked ship sank into the sea, landed safely in New York City last night about 8 o'clock, when the Carpathia, of the Cunard Steamship Line, docked with its freight of 600 people, all that were saved from the Titanic.

Immediately advices came to this city announcing they were well and safe.

the Titanic is one of the first boats, but whether he and Mrs. Bishop got separated is not known.

According to the newspaper stories the first few life boats only carried men passengers. After that the crew drove remaining men back

Mr. and Mrs. D. H. Bishop

ABOVE
The US Senate Inquiry examined witnesses of the sinking for 18 days.

She was then dismissed and Dickinson took the stand. He was asked whether he had heard any order from the crew that men should stand back and let women and children get on the lifeboats first. 'No, absolutely not,' he said firmly.

This was already a sensitive subject for Dickinson: some newspapers had been berating the male survivors for a lack of gallantry. However, although the crew members are widely reported to have insisted on prioritizing women and children at the launch of the port lifeboats, it seems Dickinson spoke the truth when he insisted that no such order was given at the launch of Lifeboat 7. The accusation of dishonour embarrassed and infuriated him in equal measure. In 1912, 'women and children first' was an established social imperative. Second Officer Lightoller went so far as to testify at the Inquiry that it was 'a law of human nature'. Dickinson Bishop had been a first-class passenger, and was, therefore, presumed to be a gentleman. People could not help asking themselves why he

OPPOSITE
(FAR LEFT)
Harold Bride, one of the Titanic's *wireless operators, is helped ashore in New York.*

(LEFT)
A newspaper article reporting the Bishops' safe return.

RUMOURS OF MEN DRESSED AS WOMEN

William T. Sloper, who had also been on Lifeboat 7, was the first man accused by the press of wearing women's clothing to secure a place. He vehemently denied it but didn't sue the newspaper in question and subsequently spent many years living down his undeserved reputation. The press then turned on Dickinson Bishop, questioning why he had been in the first lifeboat and hinting he may also have been in disguise. Many more male survivors were accused of dressing as women, but there is only one confirmed story. Daniel Buckley, a third-class passenger from County Cork, Ireland, testified to the Inquiry that when Lifeboat 13 was being loaded, several men had jumped aboard. Crew members drew guns and ordered the men off so that more women could board. Daniel, who was already on board, said that he burst into tears and a kindly lady threw a shawl over him. The other men were forced to leave, but the crew mistook Daniel for a woman. Thus, his life was saved by his disguise.

had saved himself and left many women to perish. The stigma only increased when some newspapers printed scurrilous rumours suggesting that, to get a place in a lifeboat, he might have disguised himself as a woman.

TRAGEDY FOLLOWS TRAGEDY

On 8th December 1912, the Bishops' child was born, a boy called Randall Walton Bishop, but to their great sorrow, the infant died just two days later. In the spring of 1913, they took a vacation in California to try to get over their grief. While there, they were caught in an earthquake. It wasn't serious, but it terrified Helen, because it seemed the second part of the Egyptian prophecy had come true: she had survived a shipwreck and now an earthquake. She was worried that the automobile accident that formed the third part of the prediction would be next.

'Don't be ridiculous,' Dickinson told her. 'It's all mumbo-jumbo.'

RIGHT
By 1914, most wealthy Americans owned cars, including Helen and Dickinson.

The marriage couldn't survive and they divorced in January 1916.

ABOVE
Dickinson Bishop, in later years. The Titanic *survivor lost two wives in tragic circumstances.*

But then, in November 1914, while Helen was travelling home from a country club dance with a group of friends, their car span out of control on a bend and crashed into a tree. Helen was thrown 25 feet and landed on her head, fracturing her skull. At first, she was not expected to live, but after an operation in which a steel plate was inserted, she was finally released from hospital some weeks later.

As can be the case with severe head injuries, Helen suffered a personality change after the accident. She irrationally blamed Dickinson for the crash and became aggressive and argumentative towards him. The marriage couldn't survive and they divorced in January 1916.

Two months later, while visiting some friends in Danville, Illinois, Helen slipped on a rug and hit her head just beside the spot where the steel plate had been inserted. She never regained consciousness and died a few days later of a cerebral haemorrhage, so fulfilling the final part of the fortune-teller's prophecy. By ghastly coincidence, her obituary was published on the front page of the *Dowagiac Daily News* alongside the story that Dickinson Bishop had married for the third time to Sydney Boyce, daughter of a Chicago publishing magnate.

Dickinson served in World War I, and moved with his third wife to Ottawa, where he occasionally played competitive golf. However, his life was overshadowed by the tragedy of the *Titanic*. Over the years, numerous articles and books questioned why he had survived, and resurrected the rumour that he had dressed as a woman to secure his place on Lifeboat 7.

PASSENGER MANIFEST

1ST CLASS

Name, ... *Albert Dick (b. 29th July 1880).*

Name, ... *Vera Gillespie (b. 12th June 1894).*

Married, ... *31st May 1911.*

Point of embarkation, ... *Southampton.*

Ticket no. .... *17474.*　　Suite, ... *B20.*

B (PROMENADE DECK.)

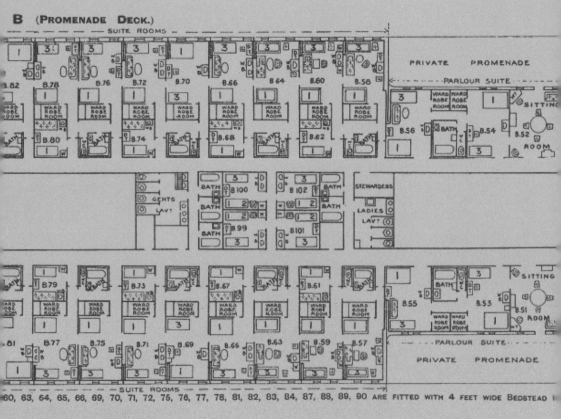

60, 63, 64, 65, 66, 69, 70, 71, 72, 75, 76, 77, 78, 81, 82, 83, 84, 87, 88, 89, 90 ARE FITTED WITH 4 FEET WIDE BEDSTEAD

Albert & Vera
Dick

Bert and Vera were often heard arguing on the ship, about his gambling and her flirtation with a handsome young steward in the first-class dining room. However, according to Vera, it was that flirtation which would save their lives.

ALBERT DICK WAS A SELF-MADE MAN, fiercely ambitious and driven to make money from a young age. With his brother, he founded a string of businesses in the province of Alberta, Canada, all before the age of thirty: a sawmill in Ponoka, a real-estate business, a hotel called the Alexandra and the three-storey Dick brothers' business building, all in Calgary. He worked hard and he played hard, developing a taste for poker and pretty women that stopped him from settling down in his twenties.

Young Vera Gillespie was only sixteen when they met, but her family was well connected and she was a pretty little thing. She hadn't been introduced into society or been much tutored in life, but that suited Bert because he thought he could mould her into the wife he wanted, someone who would be an asset in his business dealings. They married in a lavish ceremony in Calgary in May 1911, but they couldn't have a honeymoon right away because of Bert's work commitments.

It was the end of the year before they were able to leave for a honeymoon, which encompassed Egypt, Italy, France and London. In Naples, Bert had a misadventure and was fleeced by professional gamblers. Vera was furious when she found out, although somewhat mollified when he let her shop in the showrooms and department stores of London for reproduction antique furniture with which to furnish the home they planned to build on their return. She was also overjoyed to hear that they were sailing back on the great *Titanic*, hoping that they might meet some of the glamorous passengers rumoured to be travelling on the same crossing. She was homesick as well. She was still only seventeen, and she missed her mother dearly.

He worked hard and he played hard, developing a taste for poker and pretty women.

OPPOSITE & ABOVE
Vera was 14 years younger than her new husband Bert, and very attractive.

ABOVE
First-class passengers boarding the ship were led down this staircase towards their suites.

EXPLORING THE SHIP

As soon as they boarded, Vera took a childish delight in exploring the first-class areas. She wanted to try everything, from the horse-riding machine in the gym to the marble bath in their private bathroom. With Bert accompanying her, she strolled up the Grand Staircase and around all the first-class public rooms, such as the Verandah Café and Palm Court, the first-class lounge, the smoking room, the reading and writing room and the reception area that led in to the dining rooms.

Vera was disappointed to discover they were not in one of the grandest first-class suites. Everyone was talking about the two millionaires' suites: B51/3/5 on the starboard side, which was occupied by the Cardeza family, and B52/4/6 on the port side, where J. Bruce Ismay, owner of the White Star shipping line, was resident. Each of these suites had a large sitting room, two bedrooms, a private bath and trunk room, as well as its own private promenade outside. Bert pointed out that these suites cost £945 (equivalent to £53,156, or $94,500, today), while their perfectly comfortable cabin had cost only £57 (about £3,200, or $5,700, today).

The Dicks didn't have a maid travelling with them, so Vera had to unpack her own clothes and hang them in the carved wooden wardrobe. On the first day on board, her primary concern was choosing what to wear for dinner that evening. She'd read in fashion magazines that the women changed four times a day on the great liners, choosing a different outfit for each activity, and that at the evening meal they would be resplendent in jewels and décolletage dress, with their hair neatly coiffed under a jewelled and feathered headband. Men would wear a tailcoat or tuxedo, with a white waistcoat and tie.

She was nervous as they walked up to the reception room that first evening, but she needn't have been. They soon got talking to fellow passengers, and Bert was introduced to Thomas Andrews, the man who had supervised the *Titanic*'s construction.

'Is she everything they say?' Bert asked Andrews. 'There's been a lot of talk in the media about her.'

'She is as nearly perfect as human brains can make her,' Andrews said, looking around him proudly. He had always resisted giving the *Titanic* the label 'unsinkable', claiming there

EXOTIC CARGO ON THE *TITANIC*

- 12 cases of ostrich feathers
- 19 cases of orchids
- A jewelled copy of the *Rubaiyat of Omar Kayyam*, a book of ancient Persian poems, inlaid with 1,500 precious stones
- 76 cases of dragon's blood (a kind of resin derived from palm trees in Malaysia and Indonesia, used as a varnish or a dye)
- 63 cases of champagne
- A 1912 Renault automobile
- A case of movies bound for the New York Motion Picture Company
- 3 crates of ancient Egyptian models destined for a Denver museum, and later rumoured by some to have brought a mummy's curse upon the ship
- 8 cases of furniture, including the Dicks'

LEFT
Fashionable women wore ornate hats throughout the day, swapping them for bejewelled headbands in the evening.

THE GRAND STAIRCASE

The Grand Staircase ascended five levels, from D Deck up to the boat deck, and it was topped by a dome of glass and iron, which allowed natural light to flood down the stairwell. The iron balustrades were adorned with gilded flowers and bronze cherubs and, at the point where the staircase divided in two, there was a large clock set in a carved panel, inscribed with the words *Honour and Glory Crowning Time*. The angelic figure of 'Honour' was depicted recording something on a tablet, her foot resting on a globe, while 'Glory' fanned her with a palm frond, a laurel wreath of victory at her feet. It was a symbolic message from the White Star Line, the ship's owners, about its mastery over time and the oceans. They meant to reassure their first-class passengers that they would speed them across the water, and that the hours were being logged under angelic supervision.

was no such thing in shipping, but it hadn't stopped the media from using the term.

The Dicks went in to dinner and, glancing around, Vera was pleased with her choice of dress. She might not have had as many jewels as some of the older women, but in her opinion, she was one of the prettiest girls there.

The steward who served them at their table was a handsome twenty-year-old boy from Southampton, called Reginald Jones. Vera asked Jones what he recommended on the menu and made conversation with him about the food and the ship. He responded politely, but Bert was annoyed with his wife. As soon as

they were on their own, he berated her for her flirtatiousness and admonished her that it was unseemly for someone in her position to fraternize with the waiting staff. As if determined not to be ordered about, Vera continued to speak in a friendly manner to Reginald Jones whenever he came to clear their plates or bring subsequent courses. As a result, according to some fellow passengers, the atmosphere between the two honeymooners was somewhat frosty.

After dinner, Bert went to have a drink in the smoking room and it was Vera's turn to be annoyed. She knew men gambled in there and she was anxious that he shouldn't lose any more money than he had in Naples. She told friends later that they argued throughout the honeymoon about his continuous gambling.

BELOW
The Grand Staircase covered by a glass dome was the focal point of the ship's opulent decor.

ASSISTED BY MR ANDREWS

On Sunday evening, Thomas Andrews invited Bert and Vera to share his table at dinner. Vera was disappointed because it meant they had a different steward waiting on them, and she found the men's conversation about the ship dull. She glanced over to the large table where a gala dinner was being held by the Wideners, with Captain Smith as the guest of honour, and wondered why they hadn't been invited to that. She wished her husband were better connected with the old-money set on board. She suspected the Dicks were looked down on as *nouveaux riches*, and she resented not being so much as introduced to the famous Astors, or to Benjamin Guggenheim and his exotic French mistress.

Bert asked Thomas if it were true that the *Titanic* was racing to get into port early. There were rumours that she was steaming along at 23 knots.

Thomas replied that they wouldn't want to get in on the Tuesday evening in the dark. They would prefer to arrive on Wednesday morning in daylight so that the waiting press photographers could get the shots they wanted. He added that their speed was only 21 or 22 knots, and the Dicks marvelled at how smooth the movement was, without vibrations.

GAMBLING ON THE *TITANIC*

There was always a card game in progress in the first-class smoking room, with its well-stocked bar, stained-glass windows with views depicting ports around the world, and Norman Wilkinson's painting *Plymouth Harbour* above the fireplace. Occupants of the smoking room played poker, whist, bridge, pinochle, cribbage or canasta, and in common with other cruise liners at the time, there were problems with professional card sharps coming on board to try to lighten the pockets of the wealthy passengers. Crew were instructed to break up the game and warn the passenger in question if they suspected any cheating, or if a known card sharp was playing, but they wouldn't always recognize them. George Brereton was one professional gambler on the *Titanic*, and he travelled under the assumed name George Brayton to avoid detection. Incorrigible to the last, legend has it that he was working on another scam on the deck of the *Carpathia* as *Titanic* survivors were ferried to New York.

LEFT *Card games were popular among all classes on board. This hand was the last dealt to one* Titanic *survivor.*

After dinner, Bert and Vera went for a stroll on deck but they didn't stay out long, finding it too bitter. Between 5.30 and 7.30pm that evening, the air temperature had dropped from 55 to 34 degrees Fahrenheit. Had they but known it, this was an indication that the ship was nearing an ice field.

ABOVE
The life-jackets were made of cork covered in canvas. There were enough on board for every passenger, but some refused to wear them.

They were already in bed and, according to Vera, they were in the middle of yet another heated argument, when they were interrupted by a noise they later described as being 'like a thunderclap'. At just after midnight, they were still in bed discussing what the cause of the noise might have been, when there was a knock on the door.

'Mr Dick, sir?' Bert opened the door to see Reginald Jones, their dining saloon steward.

'I wanted to warn you and your wife that the ship has had a collision,' Jones said. 'The captain is asking all passengers to come up on deck wearing their life-jackets.'

'Good God, man. Is it serious?'

'I think they want you to go off in the lifeboats, as a precaution. Be sure to dress warmly, sir.'

Bert and Vera did as Jones suggested, pulling on warm woollen suits and overcoats, then picking up their life-jackets before making their way to the boat deck. They saw other passengers wandering around, uncertain what to do, and were reluctant to join the few who were climbing into the wooden lifeboats ready to be lowered over the side of the ship. It would be freezing on the open water and surely treacherous. They wondered if it would be safer to stay on board the ship.

When Bert spotted Thomas Andrews, he hurried over. 'What's the situation?' he asked. 'Should we get in a lifeboat?' Thomas Andrews led them immediately to Lifeboat 3, which was being loaded by First Officer Murdoch on the starboard side of the ship. 'More passengers for you, sir,' he said, before bidding them farewell.

ABOVE
*There was no panic as
the first lifeboats were
loaded. It was all
conducted in an air
of civilized calm.*

Reginald Jones reappeared beside them. 'Put your life-jacket on, ma'am,' he said to Vera. 'It's the latest thing this season.'

Vera didn't want to get into the boat, dangling so high above the black, cold water, but Fifth Officer Lowe coaxed her. 'Get in, Mrs Dick,' he said. 'We'll be back for breakfast.'

Reginald Jones took her elbow and helped her into the boat. Bert said later that he kissed her good-bye but she clung to his hand. Officer Murdoch was calling for more women at the time, but none would get in, so he put his hand on Bert's shoulder and pushed him towards his wife.

Surprised, Bert took a seat and looked around. Although predominantly women, there were other men in the group, including Mr Thomas Cardeza, one of the party staying in a millionaire's suite, and Mr Frederic Spedden, a keen yachtsman with whom he had chatted in the smoking room one evening. First Officer Murdoch had loaded all the women who were willing and then, finding the boat half empty, decided to allow men as well, including around ten firemen. The boat was lowered at 1am. There was some drama because the ropes got tangled, threatening to tip them all into the water. Vera clutched Bert's arm tightly and shivered in fear.

OPPOSITE
*This photograph, taken
near the location on
15th April, may show
the iceberg that sunk
the* Titanic. *There was
a smear of red paint on
its base.*

IN LIFEBOAT 3

As the crewmen of Lifeboat 3 rowed away, the blackness of the still water contrasted with the brilliant white of the stars above.

'I have never seen such a sky,' Vera whispered to Bert, 'even in Canada, where we have such clear nights.'

The occupants of Lifeboat 3 could only watch in shock as the massive ship sunk ever lower in the water, each row of cabin lights disappearing in turn beneath the surface. The bow vanished, the great stern rose into the air, and the *Titanic* began its inexorable slide. They heard the unforgettable noise of over a thousand people groaning and crying out as they plunged into the freezing ocean.

Lifeboat 3 was some distance away when the ship went down and no one suggested going back for survivors. In the hours that followed, they remained isolated, although occasionally they saw the glow of a lantern tied to the mast of another lifeboat. They had no lantern themselves, and one of the men lit matches so they could check the time. A mother and daughter – Mrs Hays and Mrs Davidson – kept calling out their husbands' names, asking desperately if anyone had seen them. The answer 'no' came back over the water every time.

WERE GUNS FIRED?

Vera later told the *New York Herald* that she heard the firing of 'several rounds of shots' and that she was told that three third-class men had been shot by an officer to prevent them from leaping onto the last lifeboat. In fact, it seems that no one was directly fired upon, but Fifth Officer Harold Lowe reported firing three warning shots to deter a crowd of what he called 'Latin-looking' passengers from jumping into Lifeboat 14, because he feared it would capsize. Two first-class passengers also reported that First Officer Murdoch fired two shots into the air during the loading of Collapsible C. Once on the *Carpathia*, a story spread among the survivors that two 'hot-headed Italians' had been shot dead by officers, and several newspapers back on shore picked up the story, which the White Star Line was understandably anxious to deny.

One woman on the boat berated herself hysterically for leaving her husband behind and had to be restrained from throwing herself into the water. Vera, clutching Bert's hand, must have realized how lucky she was to have him beside her. She knew she would have fallen apart without his solid presence by her side to protect her and make sure she was all right. She huddled against him to shelter from the biting cold.

At 4am, the faint glow of dawn appeared in the sky, then a man's voice called, 'A ship! Look, a ship!'

Someone set fire to a newspaper to draw attention to their boat, but it quickly burned. Mrs Davidson offered her straw hat, and this smouldered nicely. The sky lightened as they rowed toward the *Carpathia*. They made out the sharp, sculpted shapes of icebergs all around them in the water as far as the eye could see.

Lifeboat 3 pulled alongside the *Carpathia* and its passengers were hoisted up in a tiny rope swing. The Dicks were among the last to board. They were handed blankets and directed to a lounge where hot drinks were being served. Having stayed calm all night, Vera collapsed in a chair and began to sob because of the horror of what she had been through and for all the women who had certainly lost their husbands.

BELOW
Some evening papers reported the disaster on Monday, 15th April, but reports were still sketchy.

BACK IN CALGARY

Once in New York, the Dicks quickly enquired after their friends on board. Vera was distressed to hear that their steward, Reginald Jones, had perished. Without his insistence, they might not have gone up on deck that night and been saved. They also heard that Thomas Andrews had made no attempt to get into a lifeboat. As the ship went down,

'Previously I thought of nothing but money … The Titanic cured me of that.'

he had behaved heroically, helping passengers to don their life-jackets and find places in boats. He was last seen standing in the smoking room gazing at the painting of the sailing boat going into Plymouth harbour. His life-jacket had been discarded on a table nearby.

A steward had asked him, 'Aren't you even going to try for it, Mr Andrews?'

He hadn't replied.

With their business in New York done, the Dicks travelled quickly back to Calgary to be reunited with their families. They couldn't escape the tabloid newspapers, however, which persisted in asking why Bert had survived when many women and children hadn't. In vain, he protested that an officer had pushed him onto the lifeboat and that he was one of almost twenty men on that boat. His reputation was further stained by accusations that he had dressed as a woman to secure his place, and it wasn't long before Calgary society stopped patronizing the Hotel Alexandra, so he decided to sell it.

Vera went on to study singing at the prestigious Toronto Conservatory of Music, and achieved some success as a singer back in her hometown of Calgary.

Bert claimed to have been changed irrevocably by the experience of being on that doomed voyage, and of sitting in a lifeboat listening to the sound of a thousand people dying in the ocean around him.

'[Previously] I thought of nothing but money,' he said in an interview with *Maclean's Magazine*. 'The *Titanic* cured me of that. Since then I have been happier than I ever was before.'

After 1912 he devoted less time to his real-estate interests and moved into the business of life insurance, perhaps calculating that people might want to protect their families in case of future *Titanic*-style disasters.

BACKGROUND
Passengers on the
Carpathia *donated spare clothing for the survivors.*

PASSENGER MANIFEST

1ST CLASS

Name, *Henry Frauenthal (b. 13th March 1863).*

Name, *Clara Heinsheimer (b. 1st December 1869).*

Married, *26th March 1912.*

Point of embarkation, *Southampton.*

Ticket no. *17611.* Suite, *C88.*

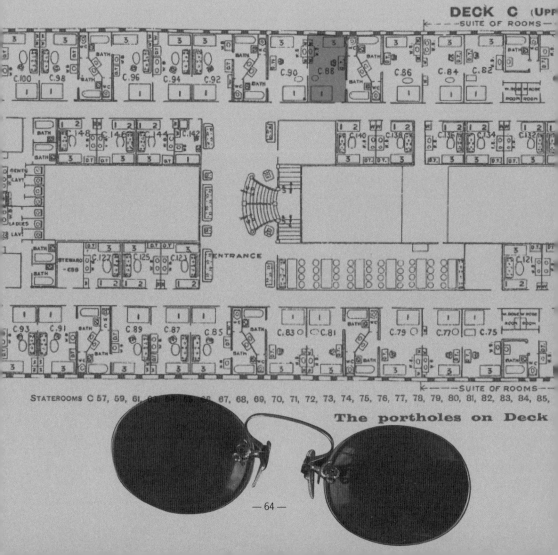

DECK C (UPP
SUITE OF ROOMS

STATEROOMS C 57, 59, 61, 62, 63, 65, 66, 67, 68, 69, 70, 71, 72, 73, 74, 75, 76, 77, 78, 79, 80, 81, 82, 83, 84, 85,

SUITE OF ROOMS

The portholes on Deck

Henry & Clara
Frauenthal

Eminent orthopaedic surgeon Henry Frauenthal was called upon to use
his skills on board the *Titanic* when a passenger broke a bone in her
arm – but he was later accused by another passenger of breaking her
ribs when he leaped into Lifeboat 5.

BOTH HENRY AND CLARA were children of German-Jewish immigrants to the United States and were brought up in well-to-do German-speaking households. In 1896, Clara married Charles Mellvaine Rogers, a partner in a grain-trading firm, in a plush ceremony at New York's finest hotel, the Waldorf-Astoria. They lived a comfortable life in Philadelphia and, in 1903, their daughter Nathalie was born, but the marriage was unhappy and, in 1906, Clara sued for divorce. This wasn't a step she took lightly because, even if permitted under Jewish law, it was frowned upon by polite society. She didn't think she would ever be able to remarry and instead devoted herself to bringing up her young daughter.

When Henry proposed, Clara couldn't believe her luck in finding love again ...

Following the death of one brother, Clara's other brother Alfred was left to administer an estate worth more than five million dollars, and he set up a nonsectarian organization, called the New York Foundation, to promote charitable and educational enterprises in the city. He was directly involved in the distribution of grants to worthy causes, and, in 1906, was one of the first to donate to the Hospital for Deformative and Joint Diseases to help fund its equipment and maintenance. Through this connection, Clara would be introduced to Henry Frauenthal, the brilliant surgeon who had founded the hospital along with his brother Herman.

Henry's career was exemplary. He attained a first-class degree in chemistry before studying medicine at Bellevue Hospital Medical College in New York and becoming an assistant to Bellevue's Chairman of Orthopaedics. At Bellevue he developed a number of new ways of treating chronic joint problems, using massage and breathing exercises, the electrical stimulation of the muscles, and machines that were able to move stiffened joints. In 1905, he and his brother set up a small, seven-bed hospital at Herman's wife's home on

OPPOSITE
Henry Frauenthal, ca. 1895, when he worked at Bellevue Hospital. He was already making a name for himself in the world of orthopaedics.

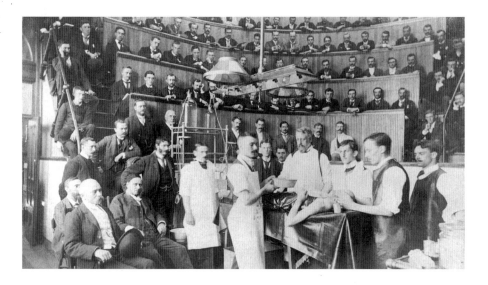

ABOVE
*An operating room,
ca. 1898, with an
audience of medical
students.*

Lexington Avenue (Herman's wife was a member of the Rothschild banking family, which had houses to spare). One year later, they opened an expanded hospital in a three-storey brownstone in Madison Avenue, with Henry as its physician and surgeon-in-chief.

Henry believed in treating the whole person, and he took patients of all ages and all races, rich and poor. During these years, he became famous for his innovative treatments of child polio victims – at a time when polio was rife and, if not fatal, likely to cause paralysis of the limbs. He was also famous for the successful graft of a tibia into the leg of a woman patient, the first surgeon in the country to perform the operation.

Henry was devoted to his career and had never considered marriage a priority. When he began to court Clara, he was forty-eight years old, short and balding, with a full red shaggy beard and moustache. Clara was forty-two with an eight-year-old daughter in tow, so it wasn't a likely match. However, the two got on well and before long the relationship developed into friendship and love. When he proposed, Clara couldn't believe her luck in finding love again, with such an eminent man.

In September 1911, the newspapers were rife with the scandal of John Jacob Astor's remarriage following his divorce. They weren't nearly as famous, but Clara and Henry wanted to avoid any negative comment on their marriage that might adversely affect his professional standing. They decided to travel to Nice in the south of France to make their wedding vows, and Henry's brother Isaac accompanied them as best man. The ceremony was romantic, if low key. Henry's work commitments wouldn't allow them a long honeymoon, but they booked a cabin on the *Titanic* for their return voyage. Henry splashed out on a superior first-class room with ensuite bathroom.

FACILITIES FOR JEWISH PASSENGERS

Anti-Jewish prejudice was widespread in the United States in the early 20th century, with some of the top hotels refusing to accept Jewish guests, but no such sentiments prevailed on the *Titanic*. There were many prominent Jewish passengers, including Benjamin Guggenheim, of that famously wealthy family; Isidor Straus, the owner of Macy's department store; Jakob Birnbaum, a diamond trader; and Samuel Goldenberg, a lace importer.

The *Titanic*'s kitchen staff included a kosher chef, Charles Kennel, and there were separate food preparation areas in the galley and pantry, where Jewish meals could be prepared. There were also Saturday prayer services. All in all, the ship's crew couldn't have been more accommodating to its Jewish guests.

Still, some of the *Titanic*'s passengers would have refused to sit down at a table with a Jewish family – the Astor family for one was notoriously anti-Semitic. However, the Frauenthals kept themselves to themselves and there are no recorded incidences of prejudice being displayed on board. Henry Frauenthal's prowess as a physician was well known on the ship and when Mrs Irene Harris tripped and fell down the Grand Staircase, breaking a small bone in her elbow,

FIRST-CLASS BATHROOMS

The *Titanic*'s first-class bathrooms had marble baths with hot and cold running seawater. As Henry Frauenthal would have been well aware, salt water was considered therapeutic for skin problems and joint pain, and many fashionable clinics and spas of the time offered thalassotherapy seawater treatments, so the *Titanic*'s designers were following a current trend. Special soap that would lather in salt water was provided, along with pitchers of fresh water with which to rinse yourself after bathing. A standpipe at the edge of the bath was operated externally, which meant you could drain your bath without having to put your hand back into the dirty water. In contrast to this luxurious set-up, there were only two baths in the third-class accommodation, meant to serve 710 passengers. In those days, people tended to bathe only once a week, so this provision was thought ample.

she eschewed the services of the ship's own doctor and insisted that Dr Frauenthal attend her. He was duly summoned, and supervised as the affected arm was set in a plaster cast.

Otherwise, Henry and Clara spent their time on board talking with Henry's brother Isaac, reading in the library or strolling along the promenade decks. Although their cabin was opposite the first-class barber's shop, Henry did not use its services to get his bushy beard trimmed, as Orthodox Judaism has precise rules about the cutting of both hair and beard.

ISAAC'S PREMONITION

Over dinner on 14th April, Isaac Frauenthal told his brother and sister-in-law about an alarming nightmare he'd had on board over two successive nights.

'It seemed to me that I was on a big steamship, which suddenly crashed into something and began to go down,' he told them. 'I saw in the dream as vividly as I could see with open eyes the gradual settling of the ship, and I heard the cries of frightened passengers.'

Henry and Clara made light of his worry. 'Maybe you shouldn't have cheese after your dinner this evening,' Henry teased. 'I think it is making your imagination work overtime as well as your gall bladder.'

Isaac's anxiety was eased by their attitude. Looking around the dining room, the other passengers seemed relaxed and happy. He decided his fears were groundless.

However, at 11.40pm that evening, when Isaac was reading in bed, he heard what he described as 'a long, drawn-out

OMENS OF DISASTER

Many omens, including Isaac Frauenthal's dream, hinted at the sinking of the *Titanic*. A cockerel crowed as it set sail from Southampton; the ship's cat abandoned ship, taking her litter of kittens with her; the *Titanic* nearly collided with another ship, the *New York*, as it pulled out of harbour; and a stoker's head was seen popping up one of the funnels at the Irish port of Queenstown, said to be a sure sign of bad luck. Many on shore claimed to have had premonitions of disaster. Around fifty people who were booked on the maiden voyage either cancelled their tickets or failed to turn up. Chief Officer Henry Wilde posted a letter to his sister from Queenstown that read, 'I don't like this ship. I have a queer feeling about it.'

rubbing noise'. Right away he got up to investigate, with the influence of the dream still fresh in his mind. He dressed and made his way up to A Deck, where he saw several first-class passengers standing around. He looked for an officer whom he could consult, and saw Captain Smith coming down the steps from the bridge. Isaac stood close enough to overhear the captain telling John Jacob Astor that the crew were loading women and children into lifeboats. He turned on his heel and hurried back down to C Deck to tell his brother.

Henry and Clara were sound asleep and he had to pound hard on their door to wake them. 'Get up!' he called. 'Quickly! It's an emergency.'

Henry opened the door, demanding to know what all the fuss was about.

Isaac told him that the ship could be sinking and they were loading women and children into the lifeboats.

Henry, who could have been forgiven for thinking his brother was having another one of his nightmares, replied, 'This boat is too big. It can't sink.'

Isaac had great difficulty in conveying a sense of urgency, but eventually his brother agreed that he and Clara would dress and go upstairs. Sure enough, on starboard deck they found the crew loading passengers into lifeboats.

Henry grumbled that it seemed an unnecessary precaution. Close by, Fifth Officer Harold Lowe was loading Lifeboat 5. 'Women and children first,' he called. 'Come quickly, please.'

THE SPHERE

AN ILLUSTRATED NEWSPAPER FOR THE HOME

THE GREATEST WRECK IN THE WORLD'S MARITIME HISTORY—THE LOSS OF THE "TITANIC"

ABOVE
Not many passengers saw the iceberg, because the ship passed it in less than a minute, but the fatal damage had been done.

MEDICAL STAFF ON BOARD

There was a surgeon on the ship, Dr William O'Loughlin, and an assistant surgeon, Dr John Simpson, as well as a small team of nurses and stewards under the command of a matron, Mrs Katherine Wallis. Their duties included conducting medical checks on all third-class passengers as they boarded to make sure they didn't have any diseases, such as consumption (tuberculosis) or trachoma, which would mean they would be refused entry to the United States at the end of the voyage. Their scalps were also checked for head lice before they were given a health certificate. The matron also kept an eye on the third-class passengers during the trip, keeping on the lookout for signs of infectious disease. There were treatment rooms for each class, a 12-bed hospital and a six-bed isolation ward, as well as a completely equipped operating room. A leaflet in the first-class cabins extolled the virtues of the medical team and reassured passengers that they would not be charged for the treatment of any illnesses they incurred during the trip, such as seasickness, and that medicines would be dispensed free of charge.

'You had better get on, Clara,' Isaac urged her. There were already several women and one little boy on the boat and the wooden seats were filling up by the minute.

Someone took Clara's arm and helped her to step across.

'But what about my husband?' she asked. 'I don't want to go without him.' She stood up to get off the boat again, but more women were being helped down and she couldn't get past them. Then she looked over the side of the boat and was petrified to see that they were suspended 70 feet above the black ocean. The sheer metal sides of the *Titanic* were as tall as an office building. Every time a new person stepped on, the boat rocked perilously from side to side.

'Henry, what shall I do?' she cried.

At that point, at 12.55am, Officer Lowe began to lower the boat. It may be that he allowed Henry and Isaac to enter at the last moment, seeing there were places empty. Another possibility is that they took their chances and jumped. According to passenger Annie Stengel, 'a Hebrew doctor' landed on top of her and a four-year-old boy, Washington Dodge Jr. She later claimed that she was knocked unconscious by the impact and that several of her ribs were broken.

In later life, neither Henry nor Isaac Frauenthal mentioned jumping into the boat or that a woman was injured on board. If a woman had been knocked unconscious, Henry would surely have tried to resuscitate her, but none of the survivors on the boat recall any such event. Mrs Stengel's husband doesn't even mention it in the newspaper interview he gave directly afterwards. The story appears to crop up for the first time in Mrs Stengel's compensation claim to the White Star Line.

Why she chose to sue the shipping company rather than Henry himself is not clear.

Once Henry and Isaac were on board, the other passengers moved up so that they could find seats near to Clara. When they reached the water, the crew rowed out until they were around 100 yards away from the ship, before they stopped to watch. It was only then, in conversation with their fellow passengers, that Henry and Clara heard that the *Titanic* had hit an iceberg and that she was going to sink.

THE SURVIVORS HEAD FOR NEW YORK

As the bow of the *Titanic* disappeared underwater, the crew of Lifeboat 5 rowed further away from the scene, worried they might be sucked under. The stern rose up, there was a pause, and then the ship slipped finally and dramatically beneath the ocean surface, accompanied by the haunting, desperate cries of all the passengers who had been hurled alive into the freezing water. As Henry later recounted, 'It seemed as if all the devils of hell had been let loose.'

Third Officer Pitman, who was in charge of Lifeboat 5, started to turn back to try to pick up survivors from the water, but several of the ladies urged him not to. They pointed out that they were almost full, and that they could all lose their lives in a futile rescue attempt.

Henry Frauenthal remained silent. He knew that by the time they had covered the distance back to where the ship had gone down, it would be too late to save any lives. No one could last long in those freezing waters. He listened with his head in his hands as the cries from the water gradually faded into silence.

BELOW
Eyewitness accounts differed, with some thinking the ship went down intact while others claimed it broke in two.

AFTER-EFFECTS OF THE TRAUMA

Of the 711 people who survived the sinking of the *Titanic*, at least seven men and one woman committed suicide later in life – a much higher rate than would be expected in the population at large. Could it be that the horrors of the night of 14th April 1912 had some influence on their decisions? In all cases, there were other contributing factors, such as debt, bereavement and marital breakdown; however, perhaps a combination of survivor guilt and the sheer awfulness of what they had witnessed contributed to their profound unhappiness. In those days, post-traumatic stress disorder had yet to be identified, and there were no counsellors in place to help the *Titanic*'s survivors come to terms with their experiences. It seems that Henry and Clara's mental health problems may have sparked Clara's daughter's interest in the subject. Nathalie studied medicine at Cornell University in New York and developed an interest in psychiatry. She travelled to Budapest in the early 1930s, where she was associated with Sigmund Freud and a colleague of his called Sandor Ferenczi.

Two hours later they were helped onto the *Carpathia*, and Henry did what he could to give medical assistance to any survivors who were unwell. He visited Madeleine Astor and found her weeping inconsolably for the loss of her husband, but otherwise not in bad health. There were remarkably few injuries to treat – people either lived or died that night.

As news of the tragedy broke in New York, Henry and Isaac's brother Edward was one of the people who thronged to the White Star Line offices. He was so overcome with emotion when he heard that they were on the survivors' list that he collapsed and had to be helped to his feet by reporters.

On the evening of 18th April, when the *Carpathia* finally docked, Henry, Isaac and Clara Frauenthal were the first passengers to disembark. They were accompanied by a young Swedish girl called Dagmar Bryhl, who had lost her brother and her fiancé and so was completely alone. She was very feeble, so Clara took her straight to the Hospital for Deformative and Joint Diseases, where she was nursed back to health.

When Henry arrived for work at the hospital the next morning, some of the younger patients greeted his approach with cheers and waving handkerchiefs. He threw himself back into his work, trying to forget what he had been through. Unfortunately, the events on board the *Titanic* would take their toll.

THE AFTERMATH

Like the other male survivors, Henry had to contend with accusations of a lack of gallantry. He countered them by claiming that when they got on the lifeboat, he and Isaac were convinced that all the women on the ship had already embarked.

Some reports commented on Henry's neat and well-kept appearance when he walked off the *Carpathia*, in contrast to the distressed state and torn, dishevelled clothing of many other survivors. There was an anti-Semitic tone in some of the press coverage and the implication of complacency must have haunted Henry, but he threw himself back into his career and achieved many notable successes over the next few years.

At home, although he and Clara tried to avoid talking about anything to do with the *Titanic*, the memories kept them awake at night. Gradually, her mental health deteriorated and Henry became increasingly depressed as he tried to help her deal with her problems. In 1927, unable to cope with the ongoing torment of his memories, plus his wife's deepening insanity, he jumped from the seventh floor of the hospital he had founded, and died instantly on hitting the ground. More than a thousand people attended his funeral, many of them former patients.

Clara was committed to a sanatorium in Connecticut, where she lived until 1943 without ever being discharged. Decades after it sank, the *Titanic* had claimed two more victims.

> *Decades after it sank, the Titanic had claimed two more victims.*

BELOW
Henry Frauenthal's New York Hospital for Deformative and Joint Diseases. In 1927, he jumped from the seventh floor.

PASSENGER MANIFEST

1ST CLASS

Name, ... *George Harder (b. 22nd October 1886).*

Name, ... *Dorothy Annan (b. 4th July 1890).*

Married, ... *8th January 1912.*

Point of embarkation, ... *Cherbourg.*

Ticket no. .... *11765.* Suite, ... *E50.*

DECK E (MAIN DECK.)

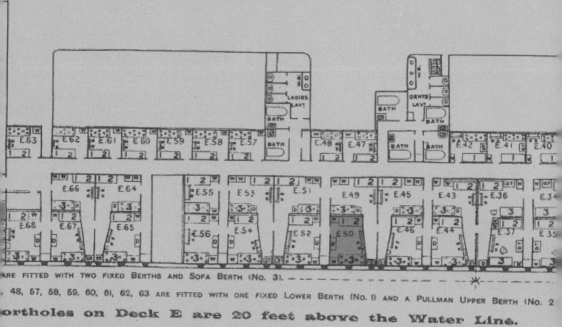

ARE FITTED WITH TWO FIXED BERTHS AND SOFA BERTH (No. 3). — — — — — — —

, 48, 57, 58, 59, 60, 61, 62, 63 ARE FITTED WITH ONE FIXED LOWER BERTH (No. 1) AND A PULLMAN UPPER BERTH (No. 2

ortholes on Deck E are 20 feet above the Water Line.

OPPOSITE
*A first-class baggage ticket that
could never be claimed.*

George & Dorothy
Harder

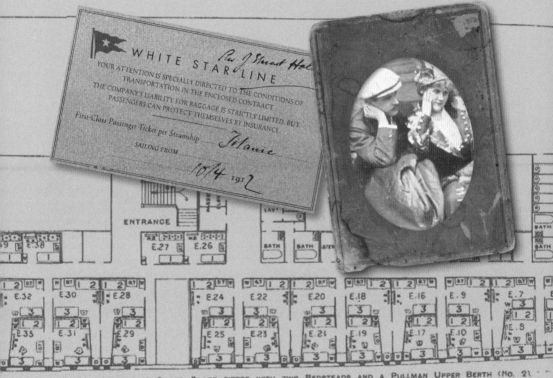

WHITE STAR LINE

Per J Stuart Hol

YOUR ATTENTION IS SPECIALLY DIRECTED TO THE CONDITIONS OF
TRANSPORTATION IN THE ENCLOSED CONTRACT.
THE COMPANY'S LIABILITY FOR BAGGAGE IS STRICTLY LIMITED, BUT
PASSENGERS CAN PROTECT THEMSELVES BY INSURANCE.

First-Class Passenger Ticket per Steamship ___ *Titanic*

SAILING FROM

10/4 1912

ENTRANCE

EROOMS WITH BERTHS NUMBERED 1, 2 AND 3 ARE FITTED WITH TWO BEDSTEADS AND A PULLMAN UPPER BERTH (No. 2)

The Harders brought a bottle of brandy onto Lifeboat 5 and offered sips to any passengers who needed reviving, then did their best to comfort the bereaved on the *Carpathia* – but afterwards it was George who needed support, because he suffered from the stigma of being a male survivor.

T HE HARDERS WERE NOT THE RICHEST or grandest passengers on the *Titanic*. They were both from successful upper-middle-class families, whose money came from trade and the professions. Dorothy's grandfather, Edward Annan, was a former president of the New York Produce Exchange and had been one of the early trustees of the Brooklyn Bridge building project. Her father had a seat on the Produce Exchange and was a manager with the Erie Railroad Company, but when Dorothy was just three years old, he collapsed and died suddenly of a stomach infection.

The family moved to Brooklyn, a prosperous borough of New York that had become more desirable after the completion of the Brooklyn Bridge in 1893. When she turned eighteen, Dorothy accompanied her sister and cousins to events thrown by the Brooklyn social set, of which her cousin, Jackson Dykman, was a prominent member. Dorothy was extraordinarily beautiful and as soon as he set eyes on her, George Harder was smitten.

OPPOSITE
George and Dorothy Harder on board the Carpathia *consoling a woman, thought to be Mrs Clara Hays, whose husband wasn't among the survivors.*

Dorothy was extraordinarily beautiful and as soon as he set eyes on her, George Harder was smitten.

BACKGROUND
At 1,596 feet, the Brooklyn Bridge was the world's longest suspension bridge from 1893 until 1903, when the Williamsburg Bridge was completed.

George was a handsome, clever young man, who worked for the Essex Foundry, which supplied metals to General Motors among others. He was a solid, reliable employee, who worked his way up the ranks and was thought by all to have a dazzling future in front of him. He'd built the career he'd sought, and now he wanted a bride with whom to start a family – and from their first meeting he was determined it was going to be Dorothy. She accepted his proposal and their engagement was announced in *The New York Times* on 31st December 1911, alongside that of his sister Hortense to Sidney Smith Whelan.

The wedding was a small, low-key affair at the home of Dorothy's cousin. Her uncle, William N. Dykman, a partner in the well-known commercial law firm Cullen and Dykman, stood in for her father to give her away. The morning after the wedding, George and Dorothy set sail for Europe, where they met up with his sister and her new husband to motor through France and Italy. They would be away for three months altogether and, as a special treat, George booked them a ticket home on the maiden voyage of the much-talked-about new ocean liner, the *Titanic*.

Dorothy was thrilled with the ship. They weren't in one of the grand suites up on B and C Decks, but their cabin was smart and they had the use of all the first-class amenities on board. It was the perfect end to a glorious honeymoon.

AN ICEBERG OUTSIDE THE WINDOW

The Harders were a sociable pair who enjoyed meeting other couples in the first-class reception room for an aperitif before dinner. There they met the Bishops, the Dicks and the Snyders, and were introduced briefly to the Astors. They chatted with the other guests about places they had visited on their honeymoon, about the ship's rapid progress across the ocean, and about what a veritable palace it was.

Everyone agreed that they kept getting lost on board. The Harders' cabin was on E Deck, so they had to walk up a floor to reach the lifts, which ran between A Deck and D Deck in front of the main staircase. Stewards spent a lot of time redirecting baffled passengers to their destinations, and even Second Officer Lightoller later reflected on the size and confusing layout of the ship: 'I was thoroughly familiar with

OPPOSITE
(TOP)
The Titanic's *gymnasium, with the rowing machine in the foreground. There was also a map on one wall showing the White Star Line's routes.*
(BOTTOM)
Bathing was strictly segregated so that men and women would not see each other in swimwear.

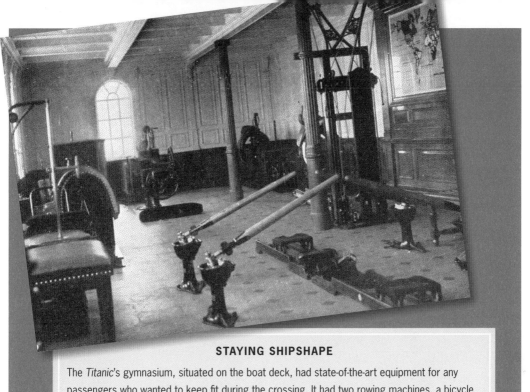

STAYING SHIPSHAPE

The *Titanic*'s gymnasium, situated on the boat deck, had state-of-the-art equipment for any passengers who wanted to keep fit during the crossing. It had two rowing machines, a bicycle racing machine, a horse-riding machine and an electric camel (a device that rotated the trunk), as well as machines that delivered a back and stomach massage. The heated seawater swimming pool on F Deck, measuring 32 by 13 feet and 6 feet deep, was open for women in the mornings from 10am to 1pm and for men from 6am to 9am and 2pm to 6pm. The Turkish baths alongside were decorated with Moroccan tilework and Egyptian lace at the windows, and tickets cost a dollar a head. Down on G Deck, there was the squash court, where tickets were 50 cents each for half an hour, including equipment rental and the services of Fred Wright, a squash professional, if desired.

THE ICEBERG FIELD

The *Titanic* was crossing the Atlantic at a latitude of 42 degrees north. As she neared Grand Banks, off the coast of Newfoundland, she sailed right into what is known to sailors as Iceberg Alley. Greenland has around twenty glaciers along its coast, and these produce around 40,000 icebergs a year, as huge portions of ice 'calve' and break off at the water's edge. One or two percent of these make it as far south as Grand Banks. Some of these are as much as 300 feet high, but around seven-eighths of them are underwater, and they are still moving south in April. During Sunday, 14th April, the *Titanic* had received several reports of icebergs, 'growlers' (the technical term for a small iceberg) and field ice, running between latitudes 41 and 49 degrees north. It is difficult to see icebergs at night, but waves lapping around them can be one sign. Unfortunately, the sea was dead calm and the *Titanic*'s lookouts only saw the misty shape appear when it was less than 500 yards away. It took the ship 850 yards to stop.

pretty well every type of ship afloat, from a battleship and a barge, but it took me 14 days before I could with confidence find my way from one part of that ship to another by the shortest route.'

George and Dorothy were a smart, well-groomed couple. George had a tidy handlebar moustache, which he had waxed and shaped at the barber's shop on C Deck. Dorothy had a fashionable hairstyle with large, soft curls held in place by a barrette, and she would most likely have slept with hair rollers in place. There were no hairdressers for women on the *Titanic*; if they didn't have a maid to do their hair for them, they did their own.

On the night of Sunday, 14th April, the Harders were in bed but not yet asleep when the ship collided with an iceberg just beneath their cabin. They heard a 'dull thump', then felt the boat quiver. George went to the porthole right away and saw an iceberg that he later described as between 50 and 100 feet tall. They heard the scraping sound of a sharp underwater spur of the iceberg on the *Titanic*'s hull. That's why, unlike many other passengers, they immediately felt a strong sense of alarm.

> *… unlike many other passengers, they immediately felt a strong sense of alarm.*

Dorothy yanked out her curlers and they both dressed themselves completely in order to be ready for all eventualities. She wore a fitted suit with contrasting buttons and embroidered panels over a neat blouse, and pinned a feathered hat to her head. George wore a wool suit and cap. The dress code in the *Titanic*'s first-class areas was so strictly adhered to that many passengers hesitated that night, wondering what the appropriate attire for a lifeboat might be.

Upstairs on the boat deck, the Harders consulted with their fellow passengers, but the general opinion was that nothing serious had happened and that the boat would be on its way again soon. George walked around the deck a few times, and that's when he noticed that the ship was listing on the starboard side. He talked to the Bishops and then the Astors, and he was there shortly after midnight when Captain Smith advised John Jacob Astor that they should go and put their life-jackets on.

OPPOSITE
At first, it was thought that the iceberg had ripped a gash in the Titanic's hull, but, in fact, it had caused the steel plates to buckle and rivets to pop out.

ABOVE
*Staterooms had a sitting
area as well as a bed,
and were individually
decorated in period styles.*

George and Dorothy went straight down to their room, where they retrieved her fur coat and his thick gabardine overcoat, a bottle of brandy and the buttonhook she used to fasten the buttons on her shoes. They were both terrified. They had believed themselves to be on the safest ship in the world, so it was an incredible turn of events.

As they came out of their room, George saw four or five crew members trying to turn a bolt in the floor, beneath a brass plate between the stairs and the lifts. He wondered if it was some kind of watertight seal, and was troubled when he overheard them saying, 'This one won't work. Let's try another one.' In fact, the watertight doors of the main bulkheads were operated electronically from the bridge and had been closed directly after the collision. The crew was probably wrestling with an individual watertight door that closed off a smaller area above E Deck, where the main bulkheads didn't reach. Seeing them only increased the Harders' sense of terror.

Breathless from running up the five flights of stairs because they didn't want to risk using the lift, they arrived on deck just in time to see the Bishops being lowered in Lifeboat 7.

Mr Ismay, President of the White Star Line, was assisting with the loading of Lifeboat 5 and he ushered the Harders towards it. The gentlemen were asked to hold back while the ladies were loaded first, then when there were no more women in sight willing to board, a few men were waved on, including George Harder. Dorothy was overcome with relief.

There were some terrifying incidents as the lifeboat was lowered. A man of Jewish appearance leaped on board, causing the craft to rock precariously, almost 70 feet above the water's surface. One side of the boat lowered faster than the other and they were all scared they were going to be tipped out. Once they reached the water, someone panicked that the plug was not secured in the bottom of the lifeboat and there was a frantic search until they realized that it was. None of the crewmen was able to detach the boat from the tackle. It wasn't until a passenger produced a knife for them to cut through it that they were able to row away from the side of the ship. Everyone's nerves were frayed.

At that point, the Harders had no idea that there weren't enough lifeboats on board for all the passengers. They had no idea that they were in the lucky minority.

BELOW
Some officers were reluctant to fill the lifeboats to capacity in case the ropes snapped while they were being lowered to the ocean.

REACHING THE *CARPATHIA*

Lifeboat 5 was rowed around a quarter of a mile from the ship and pulled up alongside Lifeboat 7. There were 36 people in the Harders' boat and 28 in the other, so four of them, one holding a baby, climbed across to even the load. None of the passengers was aware that these boats were designed to hold up to 65 people each. After the *Titanic* sank, they didn't attempt to go back

CONFUSED MEDIA REPORTING

There was confusion in the reporting of the accident in New York on Monday, 15th April. A ship called the *Baltic* sent out a message asking 'Are all *Titanic* passengers safe?' at the same time as a ship called the *Asian* sent a message that she was towing a stricken tanker back to port in Halifax. Somehow the messages got scrambled and misread ashore as '*Titanic* passengers safe; being towed to Halifax.' Some newspapers ran with that headline on Monday the 15th. In the absence of hard facts, they reported the names of the millionaires on board, and any known statistics about the 'unsinkable' ship. White Star offices were besieged by throngs of relatives seeking news, but it was 6.15pm on 16th April before they received firm confirmation via the *Olympic*: '*Carpathia* reached *Titanic*'s position at daybreak. Found only boats and wreckage … About 675 souls saved, crew and passengers, latter nearly all women.'

RIGHT *A Marconi-gram from the* Carpathia, *sent by Dr Washington Dodge to his son Harry informing him that he had survived.*

and pick up survivors from the water because they didn't think they had any room. They had no idea that the 20 lifeboats and collapsibles launched from the *Titanic* that night could have accommodated almost another 500 survivors had they been evenly distributed.

George later described the cries of those in the water as 'a sort of continuous yelling or moaning' far in the distance. He thought they sounded hysterical. He handed around his brandy on Lifeboat 5 to revive those in need of it, and they all huddled together for warmth until at last dawn broke and they saw the *Carpathia* on the horizon. It was at that stage they realized there were as many as ten icebergs in the water around them.

It took some time to row to the *Carpathia* and it was completely daylight when they were finally lifted on board. There was a grim silence as passengers who had already come aboard scanned the new arrivals for friends, family and spouses. Many women still hoped their husbands had been saved by other ships, although some broke down as the last lifeboat (Lifeboat 16) was unloaded. The *Carpathia* circled the area but there was little to be seen in the water at that time, apart from a few pieces of broken deckchair and a single body.

The *Titanic* survivors sat wherever they could find a space on their rescue ship, wrapped in blankets or coats donated by *Carpathia* passengers. Few spoke as they were all in shock. George and Dorothy made their way around, comforting the many grieving widows. Dorothy must have been thinking, 'There but for the grace of God go I.'

The *Carpathia*'s chief purser toured the decks and public rooms compiling a list of survivors. The lists were carefully checked and rechecked before being taken to the wireless operator Harold Cottam for transmission back to port.

It was Tuesday, 16th April when Dorothy's uncle, William Dykman, managed to get news from the White Star Line office that George and Dorothy were safe. He sent word to George's parents, but his mother was in such a state that a doctor had to be called. She refused to be consoled until she could see the couple with her own eyes.

Conditions were difficult on the *Carpathia* during the four days' sail. There were already 743 passengers on board and room had to be found for another 711. Cabins and bathrooms

ABOVE
Passengers crowded the decks to watch as the Carpathia *pulled into port in New York on 18th April.*

THE RESULTS OF
THE INQUIRIES

The American inquiry took place immediately after the sinking, in April 1912, and a British one took place between May and July. As a result of their findings, many new maritime laws came into force. From then on, every ship had to guarantee a lifeboat space for every passenger, and mandatory lifeboat drills came into force. Shipboard radios had to be manned for 24 hours a day, and a special maritime radio frequency was designated. All ships were fitted with searchlights and followed a more southerly transatlantic route than the *Titanic* had taken. In 1914, an International Ice Patrol was formed to monitor and advise ships of all iceberg sightings in the North Atlantic.

were shared with strangers, extra sittings had to be arranged for each meal in the dining room, and all the *Carpathia*'s third-class passengers were squashed up at one end of the ship to free up extra berths. Everyone chipped in, donating spare clothing, toiletries and toothbrushes, and no one complained. The survivors were all devastated, and couldn't wait to set foot on dry land.

There was widespread disbelief among those rescued. 'There must be another ship bringing back survivors,' everyone said. 'This can't be all of us. Surely John Jacob Astor must have survived?' Dorothy clung to George as she watched other wives searching frantically for their husbands.

It was only when the *Carpathia* berthed in New York on the Thursday evening that they learned the truth. There were no more ships. No one else had been saved. They were the only survivors of the sinking of the *Titanic*.

THE SENATE INQUIRY

When George was asked to appear at the US Senate Inquiry into the sinking, he was glad of the opportunity to tell his story, at least in part to demonstrate that in getting onto Lifeboat 5 he was simply following orders from the *Titanic*'s crew. He strongly rejected any suggestion that their boat was only half full and could have gone back to pick up survivors.

'They say those boats hold 60 people, but we had only the number of people I have mentioned [31]; and, believe me, we did not have room to spare.' Later, he added, 'I never paid any attention to how many lifeboats there were. I did not know.'

When they heard the full story of what had happened that night, the survivors were full of admiration and gratitude for Captain Rostron and his decision to turn the *Carpathia* around and speed to their rescue through an iceberg-strewn ocean. If it had not been for his instant reaction, many more would have died. George got together with half a dozen other survivors to organize a thank-you tribute to the Captain and the *Carpathia*'s crew. They had begun making a collection while still on board and, with the help of later donations, had a silver cup engraved for the Captain and 320 gold medals struck for distribution to the crew.

> *'I never paid any attention to how many lifeboats there were. I did not know.'*

After dropping the survivors off in New York, the *Carpathia* had continued on her journey to the Mediterranean, but when she made her first return visit to New York on 29th May, a special presentation ceremony took place. Frederick Seward, chairman of the survivors' committee, made a speech expressing in glowing terms the gratitude they all felt for the captain's extraordinary heroism. The captain said in turn that he could not take credit, but thanked his crew for their valour and dedication beyond the call of duty.

Perhaps taking part in this moving ceremony helped George Harder to come to terms with his feelings, but he was still troubled by the stigma of being a male survivor. Although the Harders were often asked to speak at conferences about their experiences that night, they refused all offers.

OPPOSITE
The Carpathia *brought 13 of the* Titanic's *lifeboats back to port. After mooring, they were stripped bare by souvenir hunters.*

PASSENGER MANIFEST

1ST **CLASS**

Name, *Daniel Marvin (b. 12th February 1894).*

Name, *Mary Farquharson (b. 30th January 1894).*

Married, *8th January 1912.*

Point of embarkation, *Southampton.*

Ticket no. *113773.* Suite, *D30.*

ECK D (SALOON DECK.)

DINING

RECEPTIO

ROOM

Daniel & Mary
Marvin

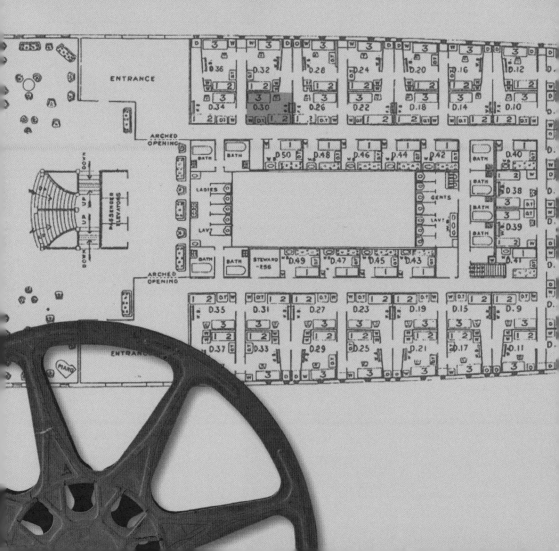

Teenagers Daniel and Mary were a familiar sight on deck, often filming each other with his big wooden Pathé camera, a wedding present from his father. They were strikingly good-looking, full of high spirits, and never spent a single moment apart – until they had no other choice.

THIS PAGE
A 1912 Kinematograph camera, with the crank handle protruding from the back.

DANIEL MARVIN AND MARY FARQUHARSON were only seventeen years old when they fell in love. Both their families thought that they were far too young to marry and advised them to wait a year or so, but the impetuous pair slipped off to New York City Hall on 8th January 1912, and married in a secret civil ceremony. They returned to their respective homes and kept their secret safe until the first week in March, by which time Mary's morning sickness was becoming impossible to hide, and required an explanation.

Once they realized the change in their daughter's circumstances, the Farquharsons sprang into action. Having a child outside a recognized marriage in 1912 would have meant the family being ostracized from the New York high society that they had worked so hard to infiltrate, so they swiftly organized a religious ceremony before friends and acquaintances could start whispering about Mary's thickening waistline. Daniel and Mary hadn't wanted a formal wedding with a lot of fuss, but they weren't given a choice in the matter.

They were married for the second time by the Reverend Dr Lyon Caughey at the Farquharson's upmarket Riverside Drive home on 12th March, before an altar covered in roses and lilies. Mary wore a lavish, multi-layered lace dress with a voluminous veil, while Daniel looked dashing in a dinner suit and white tie, his dark hair

ABOVE
Young, privileged and madly in love, Mary and Daniel Marvin sneaked off and got married in secret.

... Mary's morning sickness was impossible to hide, and required an explanation.

THE BIOGRAPH COMPANY

America's oldest movie company was founded in 1895 by an inventor called William Kennedy Dickson, who used to work at Thomas Edison's laboratory. He teamed up with three partners, one of whom was Harry Marvin, to manufacture the 'Mutoscope', in direct competition with Edison's Kinetoscope. In the summer of 1896, they then launched a projector that enabled much better image quality than Edison's, and the legal battles began. Pioneering director D. W. Griffith joined the Biograph Company in 1908 and shot many of his early movies with them, as did silent stars Mary Pickford, Lillian Gish and Lionel Barrymore. It was Daniel Marvin's ambition to become a director himself, and the plan was that on their return from Europe he would start work for the family firm.

BELOW
A Cinephote camera, ca. 1910. Turning the handle moved the film forward.

swept back from his forehead. The pair made a handsome couple.

Immediately after the ceremony, the Marvins were made to re-enact it for a hand-cranked movie camera, supplied by the Biograph Company owned by Daniel's father and operated by Daniel's uncle, Arthur. It may have been the first wedding ever to be filmed. Despite their initial wish for a no-frills ceremony, Mary and Daniel ended up having three weddings altogether.

HAPPY FAMILIES

Mary's parents, Mr and Mrs Frank Farquharson, came from Edinburgh and had flourished on arrival in New York, especially through their Fifth Avenue dressmaking business, Farquharson & Wheelock, which was run by Mrs Farquharson and her sister. Every fashionable New Yorker yearned to get married in one of their dresses, and young Mary often wore their designs to the society events she attended. In 1910/11, she was listed as a debutante in the New York Social Register, a directory of the city's elite. This was an honour that only wealth and a sufficiently upper-class background could buy.

Daniel's father, Harry Marvin, was a pioneer of motion pictures and a direct competitor of Thomas Edison, with whom he fought many lawsuits over patents. He was passionate about film, so it is little wonder that he arranged for his son's wedding to be captured on celluloid. He also gave the couple a movie camera to take with them on their honeymoon voyage, and Daniel's uncle, Arthur, gave him a lesson on how to operate it.

The camera in question was a Pathé 1909 hand crank, a cumbersome contraption housed in a wooden box with a winding handle on the side. The operator had to turn the handle at a particular speed while filming, and the custom of the day was to sing the song 'Daisy, Daisy, give me your answer do' at the same time, matching the cranking to the rhythm of the song. Was this what Daniel sang as he filmed his new wife on board the *Titanic*, or did he have a more romantic song with which to serenade her?

THE HONEYMOON

On 13th March, Daniel and Mary boarded the famous ocean liner *Mauretania* to sail to Britain for a five-week honeymoon. During their time there, they looked up some of the Farquharson relatives who had remained behind when Mary's parents emigrated. The couple listed their address while in England as 58 Acre Lane, Brixton, which at the time was a respectable but not especially fashionable district of South London. They travelled elsewhere in Europe as well, and Daniel used the camera given to him by his father to film Mary at various landmarks along the way. She enjoyed wearing some of the fabulous outfits her mother had supplied for her trousseau.

Mary was still only three-and-a-half months pregnant and it was not yet obvious when they boarded the *Titanic* at Southampton on 10th April for the voyage home. They had a first-class ticket, costing £53 and 2 shillings (about £3,030 today, or $4,550), and were allocated to cabin D30, on the same level as the first-class dining room. Daniel was filming from the boat deck as they pulled out of port, and captured on

ABOVE
An evening outfit from 1912. Mary Marvin's trousseau contained many lavish creations from her mother's dressmaking business.

celluloid the moment when the *Titanic* almost collided with another ship, the *New York*, which had come loose from its moorings – quite a coup for an aspiring young filmmaker.

Daniel and Mary would have found the *Titanic*, with its plunge pool, squash court, gymnasium and Turkish baths, more luxurious than the six-year-old *Mauretania*. Young people in first class tended to gather during the day in the Café Parisien, with its wicker chairs and big picture windows looking out across the ocean. Meals could be eaten there, and in good weather the windows would be thrown open so you could dine alfresco, accompanied by the music of the ship's resident trio, which included a French cellist and a Belgian violinist. However, although the company was congenial, Daniel and Mary were madly in love and preferred to keep to themselves, exploring the ship and filming with Daniel's camera. Several survivors later recalled seeing them embracing on deck, always completely wrapped up in each other.

On the evening of 14th April 1912, Mary and Daniel joined the other first-class passengers for a lavish ten-course meal in the first-class dining room. They sat at a table together, chatting excitedly about the home they planned to buy on their return to New York, his intended career with his father's

BELOW
The Café Parisien was designed to have the atmosphere of a French pavement café.

movie company and the nursery they would decorate for their new baby. They were full of plans for an exciting future.

THE COLLISION

Daniel and Mary were in their cabin when the *Titanic* struck the iceberg. They were not especially alarmed at first. The first-class cabins were amidships and experienced less motion than elsewhere on board. A steward knocked on their cabin door at around 12.25am, 45 minutes after the collision. He explained that there had been an accident and that they were loading passengers into lifeboats as a precautionary measure, so they should make their way out onto the deck wearing their warmest clothes. Mary cried out in panic but Daniel calmed her, reminding her of all the articles in the press that said the *Titanic* was the safest ship ever built, specifically engineered to be unsinkable.

Mary draped her fur coat around her shoulders and Daniel had the forethought to unload the reel of film from his camera before they made their way out to join the group of first-class passengers waiting on deck. At that stage, they still thought the lifeboats were more a precaution than a necessity. Then a steward started shouting, 'Women and children over here!' and Daniel urged Mary to go.

'I don't want to leave you,' she said. 'I'll stay with you so we can go together.'

'It's all right, little girl,' Daniel replied. 'You go. I will stay.'

Blinded by tears, Mary let the steward help her into Lifeboat 10. The ship was listing by this stage and there was a gap of about two-and-a-half feet to jump across. Mary twisted her ankle on landing and cried out in pain. Another woman, in a black dress, slipped

FIRST-CLASS DINNER MENU, 14TH APRIL 1912

First Course
Hors D'Oeuvres
Oysters

Second Course
Consommé Olga
Cream of Barley ·

Third Course
Poached Salmon with Mousseline Sauce, Cucumbers

Fourth Course
Filet Mignons Lili
Sauté of Chicken, Lyonnaise
Vegetable Marrow Farci

Fifth Course
Lamb, Mint Sauce
Roast Duckling, Apple Sauce
Sirloin of Beef, Chateau Potatoes
Green Pea, Creamed Carrots
Boiled Rice
Parmentier & Boiled
New Potatoes

Sixth Course
Punch Romaine

Seventh Course
Roast Squab & Cress

Eighth Course
Cold Asparagus Vinaigrette

Ninth Course
Paté de Foie Gras
Celery

Tenth Course
Waldorf Pudding
Peaches in Chartreuse Jelly
Chocolate & Vanilla Eclairs
French Ice Cream

RIGHT
Some lifeboats narrowly avoided colliding with each other as they were lowered to the water.

OPPOSITE
Francis Browne, a trainee priest who disembarked at Queenstown, took this photograph of six-year-old Douglas Spedden playing on A Deck, watched by his father. Both survived, but Douglas was killed in a car accident three years later.

and fell between the ship and the lifeboat and had to be pulled to safety by men on the deck below. Children were being thrown in by the crew and caught by passengers. No one panicked but the sense of urgency was apparent.

Once Mary was seated, Daniel tossed her the reel of film. Perhaps by that stage, having seen the chaos all around him, he realized that there was a chance he might not make it. The reel would have been held in a circular can, probably six inches across and three inches deep – a fairly hefty object for his pregnant wife to carry. Daniel, with the movie industry in his blood, may have wanted to ensure his record of life on board survived, even if he didn't.

As their boat was lowered, Mary saw a passenger forcing his way into a lifeboat by brandishing a revolver. She was terrified. Looking down from on deck, Daniel blew her a kiss.

THE FATE OF THE CHILDREN

There were 127 children on board the *Titanic*, of whom 54 died when the ship went down. Only one of the dead – Helen Louraine Allison, two years of age – was a first-class passenger. Her baby brother, Trevor, had been taken on another lifeboat by their nurse, but her parents didn't realize this and vowed to stay on the *Titanic* until they found him. The three of them perished. The remaining 53 children had all been travelling third-class; only 23 third-class children survived. At least twelve of the women passengers on the ship were pregnant. One had a miscarriage and two had babies who died shortly after birth, but nine of them, including Mary Marvin, went on to give birth to healthy children. These children were, in effect, also survivors of the *Titanic* disaster.

Just as Lifeboat 10 neared the water, a Turkish man called Neshan Krekorian, who had been travelling in third-class, leaped over the side of the ship and landed in their boat, badly bruising a woman's leg. Everyone berated him, reminding him that the lifeboat was only for women and children.

There were three young children and a nine-week-old baby on Lifeboat 10. The baby, Millvina Dean, became the youngest passenger to survive the disaster. All the other occupants of the lifeboat were women, apart from the two crewmen and Neshan Krekorian. Krekorian refused to leave the boat, and Mary could not help wishing that her own husband had not been such a gentleman, and had also forced his way on board.

The lifeboat was rowed about 200 yards from the sinking ship, with Mary all the while straining her eyes, desperately scouring the deck on which she had last seen Daniel and praying that he had safely got into one of the other lifeboats. When the ship's great hull finally slid under the water at 2.20am, she covered her face and began to sob uncontrollably. The crewmen tied up their lifeboat to three others, and the 31 passengers on Lifeboat 10 huddled together. Fifth Officer Harold Lowe distributed the passengers from his boat, Collapsible D, among the four, then rowed back to look for survivors. They stayed like this until the *Carpathia* arrived and they were helped on board by their rescuers.

BELOW
Survivors pose for a photograph on the Carpathia. *The woman in the fur coat is Lady Duff Gordon, and with her are her husband and secretary. They were accused of commandeering Lifeboat 1 for their own use.*

CROWD AWAITING SURVIVORS FROM "TITANIC"

LEFT
*Relatives and
friends anxiously
await the arrival
of the* Carpathia
in New York.

ALONE IN NEW YORK

Mary wandered the decks of the *Carpathia*,
desperately searching for her husband and
refusing to take any food or coffee. After
Captain Rostron had a list of passengers
compiled, she could be pretty sure that Daniel
wasn't on board. She was beside herself with
grief. The other passengers tried to console her
by saying there must be other ships, and that
she would find him once back in New York.

Both Mrs Farquharson and Mrs Marvin
were waiting at the port when the *Carpathia*
docked in New York on 18th April. Mary ran
straight into her mother's arms.

'Is he here yet?' she cried. 'Is Daniel here?'
They went to enquire at the White Star Line
office, where they were able to consult the
Carpathia's list of survivors. When Mary was
finally told by an official that her husband had
not been in any of the lifeboats and that there
was, therefore, no chance he was still alive,
she fainted. Her mother waved smelling salts
under her nose to revive her and as Mary came
round she cried, 'He blew a kiss at me. That
was the last I saw of him.'

A HONEYMOON COUPLE ON THE *CARPATHIA*

Passengers on the *Carpathia* were
asleep when their ship, originally
bound for the Mediterranean,
changed course and headed north
at full speed. Some noticed the
increased engine vibrations, and
as the truth about their rescue
mission leaked out, a number of
passengers came out on deck to
watch from the railings. Among
them were a honeymoon couple,
James and Mabel Fenwick, on their
way to begin a three-month trip in
Europe. They had a camera with
them and took many photographs
of the icebergs in the waters of
the North Atlantic, of the lifeboats
drawing alongside the *Carpathia*
and of the shocked survivors
recovering on board. They could
have had no idea at the beginning
of their voyage that they would be
partial witnesses to one of the
most devastating disasters in
the history of steamships.

Still Mary hoped that her husband's body might be found, so that he could be given a proper burial. It never was. No one knows what happened to Daniel Marvin in his final minutes. He may have found a piece of wreckage to cling to when the ship went down, but perished in the freezing waters of the Atlantic before the *Carpathia* could reach him. He may have been hit by the *Titanic*'s great funnel, or trapped and pulled down with the ship.

Mary spent the remaining months of her pregnancy in deep mourning. To go from the intensity of first love to widowhood at the tender age of eighteen was more than she could bear. She couldn't face looking at their wedding footage or any other reminders of happy times. On 21st October, she gave birth to a daughter, Mary Margaret Elizabeth Marvin, the only child Daniel would ever have, and was grief-stricken yet again that this little girl would never know her father.

REMARRIAGE

By the summer of 1913, Mary had recovered from her grief sufficiently to attend some of the season's high society social events, including the Poughkeepsie races, where she was seen with Horace S. De Camp, a friend of the Farquharson family. Their friendship deepened over the next few months and on Christmas Day 1913, Mary and Horace were married in front of 800 guests at the Harlem Presbyterian Church. The bride wore a white velvet outfit trimmed with sable, and her flower girls and page boys sprinkled white rose petals in her path.

One person who was not invited to the wedding was the actress Florence E. Clark. In 1914, Florence issued a $50,000 lawsuit against Horace De Camp for breach of promise, claiming that he had been engaged to her in 1913. She had apparently given up her stage career to prepare herself for becoming his wife, before his head was turned by Mary Marvin. De Camp countered that there was no written agreement and questioned her story on several particulars, before the matter was settled out of court.

After their wedding, Mary and Horace sailed to Egypt for a three-month honeymoon. Upon their return, they moved into a house he had bought in Great Neck, Long Island. In 1916, Horace adopted the child Mary had borne Daniel, who was

OPPOSITE
A life of glamour, premieres and stars – a life Mary could only dream about.

known to all as Peggy, and they went on to have two more children together – a daughter named Julia and a son, Frank.

Horace was a property speculator and they lived well, with a spacious home and also a country retreat. However, Mary sometimes looked at magazine pictures of Hollywood stars and speculated about the glamorous life she could have led as the wife of a movie director. If only Daniel had found a way onto a lifeboat.

THE HONEYMOON MOVIE

The fate of the honeymoon movie remains a mystery. Did Mary bring it back to New York with her? One theory is that she gave it to Daniel's father, and that it was placed in the archives of the Biograph Company. Another anecdote relates that Mary rowed out into the middle of a lake and threw it overboard, because she couldn't bear to be reminded of how happy she had been on her honeymoon with Daniel, her first love. If the movie was ever to turn up, it would be one of the greatest historical treasures to have survived the *Titanic* tragedy, and would no doubt inspire a new movie in the Hollywood hills, where Daniel Marvin's father helped to found a movie-making industry.

Mary speculated about the glamorous life she could have led as the wife of a movie director.

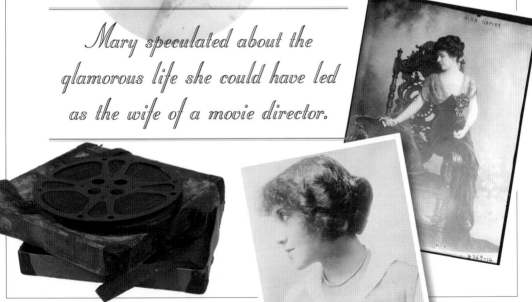

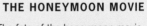

PASSENGER MANIFEST

1ST CLASS

Name, *Victor Peñasco y Castellana*
(b. 24th October 1887).

Name, *Josefa (Pepita) Perezde de Soto y Vallejo*
(b. 3rd September 1889).

Married, *8th December 1910.*

Point of embarkation, *Cherbourg.*

Ticket no. *17758.* Suite, *C65.*

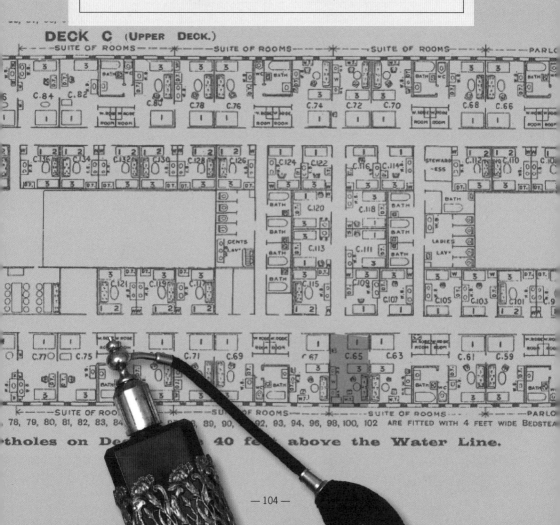

Victor & Pepita Peñasco

Being evacuated from a sinking ship was terrifying for everyone, but perhaps even more so for those passengers who didn't speak English. Pepita and Victor struggled to understand what was going on – and then they were separated.

THIS PAGE
Their extravagant two-year honeymoon saw the Peñascos tour some of the most fashionable destinations, including Monte Carlo and Vienna.

THEIRS WAS THE MOST LAVISH HONEYMOON of any of the newlyweds on the *Titanic*. It was planned to last two years, while building work was carried out on their home: a huge *palacete* in Madrid comprising three storeys, 44 terraces and every extravagance that money could buy. Before they boarded the *Titanic*, Victor and Pepita's travels took them to Vienna, where they had their own box at the opera; to Monte Carlo, where they gambled at the casinos; to London, where they enjoyed shopping; on the *Orient Express* to Venice; and then back via Biarritz to Paris. At every place they stopped, they stayed in the very best hotel, and Victor bought Pepita an exquisite piece of jewellery.

> *Victor's mama had had a premonition that an ocean voyage would bring bad luck, and made them promise to avoid boats.*

Whenever the couple was running low on money, Victor's mama would send another draft from his trust fund. They had soon spent over £10,000, a huge amount for the day (about $1 million today), but there was plenty more where that had come from. Victor's fortune had been passed down from his grandfather, the first minister to King Alfonso XIII, and father, a successful author. He himself had never done a day's work in his life, because he never needed to. Pepita also came from a wealthy family – her uncle was the Premier of Spain – and she enjoyed the good life, with servants to wait on her every whim.

While staying at Maxim's in Paris in March 1912, Pepita and Victor couldn't help seeing the posters advertising the *Titanic*. It sounded divine. The biggest ship in the world, the most luxurious ... these words appealed to young Victor and Pepita. Besides, they yearned to see New York. Their only problem was that mama had forbidden them from setting foot on a ship. She had had a premonition that an ocean voyage would bring bad luck, and made them promise to avoid boats.

ABOVE
Pepita's maid, Fermina Oliva y Ocaña, who had a room on the Titanic *just opposite the Peñascos.*

RIGHT
*Prolific billboards
proclaimed the* Titanic
*to be the biggest and
the best.*

Victor's mama was old-fashioned. She saw omens and portents in everything. Why, they reasoned, should they listen to her? So, in great excitement, they sent their manservant, Eulogio, to enquire about tickets. He booked them a superior first-class cabin costing £108 (equivalent to £6,075, or $10,800, today), with a smaller room just across the hall for Pepita's maid, Fermina Oliva y Ocaña. Eulogio could not accompany them because he was needed in France to carry out their deception. They wrote a pile of postcards to their families, rhapsodising about their stay in Paris, and Eulogio was to mail one every week, so that no one would ever suspect they had left dry land. It was perfect. They could get to New York and back and their families would be none the wiser.

Eulogio may have felt aggrieved to be left behind when they set off to board ship on 11th April, but soon he would feel very lucky indeed.

THE LITTLE CANARIES

Pepita was enchanted by the ship. Although she'd been used to luxury all her life, this was something particularly special. 'It was all incredibly beautiful,' she said, 'and the people? Well, the crème de la crème of the entire world.'

It was the little touches that separated the *Titanic* from other liners of the day. Fresh flowers were kept in cold storage so that there was always a new bouquet when an old one started to wilt; the promenade deck was enclosed in glass so first-class passengers could look out to sea without fear of being splashed or rained upon; there were five grand pianos; a darkroom enabled amateur photographers to develop their own shots; the Verandah Café even had real palm trees in it. No wonder the *Titanic* was called 'the millionaires' special'.

The other first-class passengers were quick to notice Victor and Pepita. The young Spaniards were good-looking, well-dressed and obviously madly in love. Helen Bishop later said, 'They were just like little canaries. They were so loving, and were having such a happy honeymoon that everyone on the *Titanic* became interested in them.' Pepita showed off her fabulous jewellery and magnificent gowns – some, from Maison Lucile in Paris, had been designed by fellow passenger Lady Duff Gordon. Because of the language barrier, however, they mainly socialized with the Argentinian and Uruguayan first-class passengers, and they favoured the Café Parisien.

BELOW
Lady Duff Gordon, who owned Maison Lucile fashion houses in London, Paris and New York, set the fashion standard on board.

After dinner on 14th April, Fermina retired to her cabin to mend one of Pepita's corsets. Pepita and Victor didn't come back to their room until 11.30pm. Pepita went straight to bed and Victor had just put his shoes outside the door to be polished by their steward, when they heard an odd noise and felt the slight bump of the collision.

Victor went upstairs and, in his halting English, asked a steward if there was a problem. The steward said there wasn't, but Victor could see that other passengers were gathering on the boat deck, so he decided to err on the side of caution.

**PASSENGER
NATIONALITIES**

The overwhelming majority of
first-class passengers were wealthy
American tourists, with the British
and Canadian contingents trailing
far behind in number. There were
also French, German, Dutch, Irish,
Swedish, Belgian, Spanish and
Swiss first-class travellers, an
Argentinian, two Uruguayans
and a Mexican. In second class,
passengers were predominantly
emigrating British couples, with
a few Europeans and some
individuals from far-flung regions
such as Japan, Russia, Australia
and South Africa. In third class, the
biggest ethnic groups were British
and Irish, but there were also many
passengers from Bulgaria, Bosnia,
Croatia, Greece, Turkey, Syria
and Lebanon. They tended to
be unpopular with the Western
Europeans, who looked down on
them for their 'poor hygiene and
manners'. In a society ruled by
class, third class was further
subdivided according to ethnicity.

He returned to the cabin and told Pepita
to come upstairs. She put a shawl over her
nightdress and pulled on some shoes while
Victor collected Fermina. He had seen some
of the other passengers carrying life-jackets
so he brought those as well.

On the port side of the boat, women were
being loaded into Lifeboat 8. Victor helped
Pepita and Fermina to board, and he assisted
a woman carrying a child in her arms. After
that, he got lost in the crowd.

'Victor? Where are you?' Pepita and Fermina
called in Spanish. Had he gone back to their
cabin to collect her jewellery? Why hadn't he
followed them onto the boat?

Pepita hadn't understood Seaman Thomas
Jones when he told Victor that only women
and children were allowed to board. She didn't
notice that the only men on the lifeboat were
crew members and had no idea why Victor
wasn't right behind her. In fact, realizing he
couldn't join his wife, he had deliberately
vanished from her sight. He wanted her life to
be saved; he didn't want to risk her clambering
out of the boat to rejoin him. It was an act of
supreme selflessness.

At 1.10am, the crew started to lower
Lifeboat 8. Pepita and Fermina screamed
at them in Spanish that they must wait for
Victor, but no one paid any attention. They
had seen a light on the horizon that they
thought must be another ship, and as soon
as they reached the water, the oarsmen started
to row towards it.

LIFEBOAT 8

There were 24 women, a seaman, two stewards and a cook
on board Lifeboat 8 – and only two of these people, Seaman
Jones and Noël, Countess of Rothes, knew how to row. The
stewards didn't even seem to realize that the oars had to go

into oarlocks, so it became clear early on that the women
would have to help. Fortunately, the Countess of Rothes was
a remarkable woman, who virtually took command of the boat.
She taught the others how to use the oars and took over the
tiller herself, steering them through the water towards the
distant light that they were sure would bring safety.

Seaman Jones didn't mind at all. He later said of the
countess, 'When I saw the way she was carrying herself and
heard the quiet, determined way she spoke to the others, I
knew she was more of a man than any we had on board.'

Theirs was only the second lifeboat to leave the *Titanic*,
and the plan was that they would reach the mystery ship,
unload their passengers, then return to collect more survivors.
However, as they rowed, they realized the other ship was
further away than they had thought – either that or it
was moving away.

Fermina and some of the other women passengers took a
turn at the oars, but Pepita couldn't stop crying out hysterically

BELOW
*Lifeboat 14, commanded
by Fifth Officer Lowe,
towing collapsible D
towards the* Carpathia.

for Victor. She was beside herself with grief and terror. In the end, the Countess of Rothes handed over the tiller to her cousin and went back to comfort the young Spaniard. Pepita sobbed helplessly in her arms.

As the *Titanic* sank behind them, the countess did her best to distract Pepita from the terrible sounds, as people jumped or were hurled into the freezing water and the colossus of a ship slid gradually under the surface. Yet Pepita saw it all. She said later, 'There was a massive noise, as if a mountain were collapsing. When I turned my head, the ship had disappeared as if it had been swallowed down some mysterious throat.'

Lifeboat 8 was half empty but too far away to be of much use to survivors. Although the countess wanted to go back, the stewards refused, as did the American women on board, who feared they would be swamped.

Pepita's only hope was that Victor had managed to get onto another lifeboat. At dawn, they sighted the *Carpathia* and as

THE COUNTESS OF ROTHES

In 1900, Lucy Noël Martha Leslie married the Earl of Rothes and moved into his 10,000-acre estate in Fife, Scotland. They had two children and led a country lifestyle, with hunting, shooting and fishing as their main pursuits. The Countess of Rothes was an attractive woman and an eccentric, slightly bossy character. She caught the *Titanic* en route to join her husband in California, where he was considering buying a citrus farm to supplement their estate income. Thomas Jones, the seaman on Lifeboat 8, was immediately taken with her. 'She had a lot to say, so I put her to steering the boat,' he explained. Later, he sent her the brass number plate from the side of the lifeboat as a token of his esteem, and the two kept up a correspondence every Christmas that lasted until her death in 1956.

*Conditions were crowded
on board the* Carpathia
*as she headed back to
New York.*

soon as Pepita got on board, she began her frantic search.
She paced every corridor and every stateroom looking for her
husband, to no avail. When the last lifeboat was unloaded, she
collapsed in a heap, sobbing loudly. Before turning to head to
New York, the *Carpathia*'s captain sailed the ship in a circle
around the site where the *Titanic* had gone down. Pepita stood
at the rail, refusing all offers of food and drink, gazing at the
ocean in the vain hope of seeing her husband. She was desperate
for a sign that he had survived, but there was none.

THE FAMILIES FIND OUT

Victor's mama was eating lunch in Madrid on Monday,
15th April, when a fly landed in her soup. 'Something is the
matter with Victor,' she said right away.

She phoned Maxim's in Paris, and was told that the couple
had checked out some days before. Mama started phoning
the Spanish embassy in every country she thought they could
have travelled to, and by Tuesday, 16th April, the embassy in
London was able to confirm that Pepita had been named
as one of the survivors of the sinking of the *Titanic*. Victor,
however, had not.

THE *CALIFORNIAN*

The *Titanic* story is littered with 'if onlys', but most poignant is that there was probably another ship, the *Californian*, between 5 and 20 miles away. This was most likely the ship Lifeboat 8 was heading for. Her radio operator had gone to bed at 11.30pm so he didn't pick up the distress calls. Several people on the *Californian* saw a ship on the horizon, and even noticed the distress rockets she sent up, but didn't know what to make of it. Officers on the *Californian* tried to signal the *Titanic* with a Morse lamp, but no one thought to go down to the radio room to make contact. Had they done so, they could have reached the *Titanic* before she sank, lowered their own lifeboats and picked up hundreds more survivors. The *Californian*'s captain, Stanley Lord, claimed they were miles away and it wasn't his ship that could be seen from the *Titanic*, but he was heavily criticized by the subsequent official inquiries.

Pepita's uncle, the Premier of Spain, called the Uruguayan ambassador in New York and asked if he would look after Pepita when the *Carpathia* docked, until her father was able to sail out to join her. The ambassador took Pepita, along with Fermina, to the Waldorf-Astoria. Still, Pepita hoped another ship might have picked up survivors, but every enquiry came to nothing. The *Californian* had finally arrived at the scene the morning after the tragedy, but found only wreckage and empty lifeboats.

When he got to New York, Pepita's father did his best to comfort her, but she refused to believe that Victor had gone. They heard that the *Mackay-Bennett* had arrived in Halifax with some bodies, so he decided to travel up there with Fermina to find out whether Victor's was among them. It must have been a terribly grim task, wandering along the rows of corpses, swollen and in the early stages of decomposition. They checked every single one, but without success. Victor wasn't there.

This raised another problem: under Spanish law at the time, if there was no body, a person couldn't be declared dead until 20 years after his or her disappearance. Pepita was only twenty-two. Without proof that her husband had died, she wouldn't be able to remarry, or inherit her husband's estate, until she reached the age of forty-two.

ABOVE
*A brass nameplate recovered
from one of the lifeboats.*

Without proof that her husband had died, she wouldn't be able to remarry ...

Mama had a solution. Money changed hands, a body was 'found' and identified by Fermina, and a death certificate was issued. There would be no grave bearing the name of Victor Peñasco in the Fairview cemetery in Halifax where other *Titanic* victims are buried, but the legal requirements had at least been satisfied.

After six years of mourning, Pepita finally remarried. She and her new husband, the Baron of Rio Tovía, went on to have three children together. Fermina continued to work for Pepita until she retired. Neither of them ever completely got over the shocking end to that 17-month honeymoon. As it had for all the *Titanic* survivors, the disaster cast an inescapable shadow over their lives.

ABOVE
Pepita as a widow. She never forgot her first love, Victor, and the way he made sure she survived the sinking of the Titanic.

PASSENGER MANIFEST

1ST CLASS

Name, *Lucian Philip Smith (b. 14th August 1887).*

Name, *Mary Eloise Hughes (b. 7th August 1893).*

Married, *8th February 1912.*

Point of embarkation, *Cherbourg.*

Ticket no. *13695.*   Suite, *C31.*

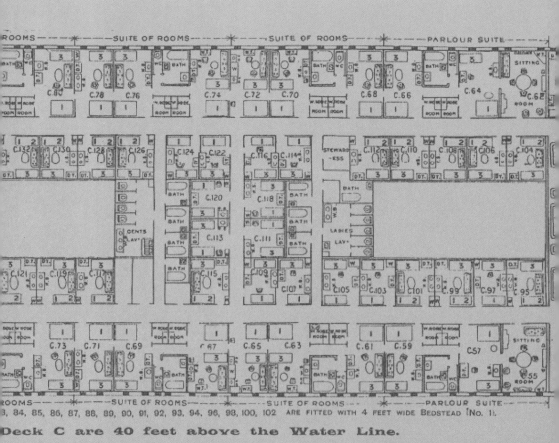

ROOMS — SUITE OF ROOMS — SUITE OF ROOMS — PARLOUR SUITE

C.80 C.78 C.76 C.74 C.72 C.70 C.68 C.66 C.64 C.62

C.132 C.130 C.128 C.126 C.124 C.122 C.116 C.114 STEWARD -ESS C.112 C.110 C.108 C.106 C.104

BATH C.120 C.118 BATH

GENTS LAV. C.113 C.111 LADIES LAV.

C.121 C.119 C.117 C.115 C.109 C.107 C.105 C.103 C.101 C.99 C.97 C.95

C.73 C.71 C.69 C.67 C.65 C.63 C.61 C.59 C.57 C.55

ROOMS — SUITE OF ROOMS — SUITE OF ROOMS — PARLOUR SUITE

3, 84, 85, 86, 87, 88, 89, 90, 91, 92, 93, 94, 96, 98, 100, 102 ARE FITTED WITH 4 FEET WIDE BEDSTEAD (No. 1).

Deck C are 40 feet above the Water Line.

OPPOSITE
*Playing cards rescued
from the* Titanic.

Lucian & Eloise
Smith

Married after a whirlwind romance and widowed two months later at the age of eighteen; gave birth to a son at nineteen, then remarried a fellow *Titanic* survivor at twenty-one – the bare facts of Eloise's young life sound like a soap opera, but the trauma she went through overshadowed the rest of her days.

Young, wealthy and attractive, the couple had everything going for them.

W HEN A UNIVERSITY CLASSMATE showed Eloise's photograph to Lucian Philip Smith, he was smitten right away and determined to meet her. He went to Huntington, West Virginia, specifically to be present at her society debut in January 1912, and he obviously made a good impression because just a month later they were married.

They both came from good families. Lucian was from Morgantown, West Virginia, where his family had substantial holdings in the area's coalfields. Eloise was the daughter of a Republican congressman in the House of Representatives and had spent much of her childhood living opposite the White House. Their marriage in Huntington's Central Christian Church was described by the press as 'one of the most brilliant wedding functions that the city ever witnessed'. Young, wealthy and attractive, the couple had everything going for them.

They sailed across the Atlantic for an action-packed honeymoon. They rode camels around the pyramids in Egypt and Lucian climbed one to the summit. They sailed to Brindisi, in the heel of Italy, travelled by rail up to Nice and Monte Carlo and then on to Paris. They even fitted in a brief trip to Amsterdam, where Lucian bought Eloise a flawless diamond. The couple were beside themselves with happiness when,

OPPOSITE
Eloise Smith with baby Lucian Jr, born seven months after his father died on the Titanic.

BELOW
The pyramids were an obligatory stop for Americans doing a European tour.

MISTRESSES ON THE SHIP

The problem with taking a mistress on a great ocean liner is that if the ship sinks, the truth is likely to come out. Benjamin Guggenheim was travelling with French singer Léontine Aubart, but when the ship was going down he made a steward promise to take a message to his wife: 'Tell her that my last thoughts will be of her and our girls.' Also in first class, Quigg Baxter was travelling with Berthe de Villiers, a Belgian courtesan, a fact his mother only discovered when he helped them both into Lifeboat 6. Quigg didn't make it to New York, where his mother promptly bought Berthe a ticket back home to Belgium. Filmmaker William Harbeck's wife's suspicions were aroused when she was told that his body had been recovered still clutching the handbag of a Miss Henriette Yrois, a twenty-four-year-old model with whom he had been travelling in second class. Yrois also drowned. Some even said that Bruce Ismay, chairman of the White Star Line, had a 'special friendship' with Edith Russell, a fashion journalist who was a passenger in first class.

towards the end of the honeymoon, Eloise discovered that she was pregnant. She wrote to her parents, telling them that they would sail home from Cherbourg 'either on the *Lusitania* or the new *Titanic*'.

History relates that they made the wrong choice. On 10th April, Lucian and Eloise were in the tender that took the multi-millionaires John Jacob Astor and his new wife Madeleine, Benjamin Guggenheim and his mistress Léontine Aubart, and George and Eleanor Widener with their son Harry out from Cherbourg harbour to board the *Titanic*.

THE HONEYMOON IS OVER

Eloise's pregnancy left her slightly unwell on the ship and she went to bed early on those few evenings, leaving Lucian to play cards with the men in the smoking room. During the days, they strolled along the covered promenades or sat in the Café Parisien discussing the life they were returning to on a farm in Huntington, where they planned to raise their family. They speculated whether the baby would be a boy or a girl – he wanted a boy first – and talked about babies' names. Every day they fell more deeply in love.

On the evening of Sunday, 14th April, Eloise and Lucian had dinner in the first-class dining room, where the Wideners were throwing a party for Captain Smith. Afterwards, they sat and listened to the band playing in the Parisien. Eloise went to bed at 10.30pm while Lucian joined three Frenchmen – Alfred Fernand Omont, Paul Chevré and Pierre Maréchal – in a game of auction bridge. At 11.40pm, the men heard a violent

OPPOSITE
Benjamin Guggenheim, heir to a family fortune made in mining, changed into his finest evening wear after the collision, explaining that he wanted to go down 'like a gentleman'.

BELOW
As the Titanic *left Southampton, she narrowly avoided a collision with the American liner* New York.

grinding noise and, looking through the portholes, saw a giant slab of ice rubbing against the ship's sides.

Instantly, Lucian was alarmed. The men hurried outside for a better view and there they overheard a woman asking one of the ship's officers what had happened.

'Don't be afraid. We are only cutting a whale in two,' he replied facetiously.

John Jacob Astor appeared on deck and, according to perhaps apocryphal reports, quipped, 'I asked for ice in my drink, but this is ridiculous.'

Everyone was peering over the rails to try to see the iceberg, crying, 'I've never seen one before. Where is it?' No one seemed to take the collision seriously. Then John Jacob Astor caught up with Captain Smith and was told that they should get their life-jackets and make their way to the boat deck, where women and children would be loaded into the lifeboats.

Lucian hurried down to their stateroom to waken Eloise. He put the lights on and stood smiling by the bed.

'We are in the north and have struck an iceberg,' he said, with nothing in his tone communicating any sense of alarm. 'It does not amount to anything, but will probably delay us a day getting into New York. However, as a matter

BELOW
Able seaman Joseph Scarrott sketched the iceberg that he had seen just after the collision and it bears a remarkable resemblance to a photograph taken the next morning, a few miles south of the Titanic's *last position.*

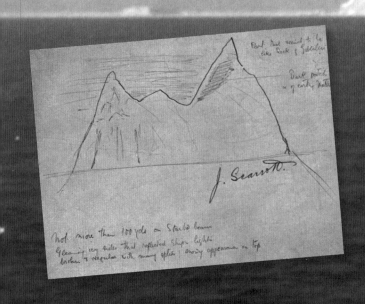

of form, the captain has ordered all ladies on deck.'

Despite his calm demeanour, Eloise was worried. She dressed in a heavy woollen dress, high-top shoes, a knitted hood and two coats. Lucian stood, talking about their plans for when they got back home. Once ready, they picked up their life-jackets and walked into the hall.

A thought occurred to Eloise, 'I should bring my jewellery.'

'Don't delay for such trifles,' Lucian quickly admonished, but she hurried into the room and grabbed her diamond from Amsterdam and ring he had bought her in Paris, then they went up together to the boat deck.

Other couples from first class were milling around and an officer told them to go down to A Deck, where the ladies would be helped into a lifeboat from the covered promenade. However, when they got there, the glass windows of the promenade were still closed and no one could board, so Lucian and Eloise took shelter in the gymnasium, where they chatted to the Astors. Eloise kept asking Lucian if she could stay with him instead of go on a lifeboat and he reassured her that she could. He went to ask for advice whenever they saw an officer go by, but as far as she was concerned there was still no call to panic.

An hour after the collision, officers began loading Lifeboat 4 through the promenade window. Madeleine Astor got in and the boat was almost full, but still Eloise refused to board without Lucian. Suddenly, she spotted Captain Smith and hurried over.

'I am all alone,' she told him. 'Please could my husband come in a lifeboat with me?'

Ignoring her, he continued to shout into a megaphone, 'Women and children first.'

'Never mind about that, Captain,' said Lucian. 'I will see that she gets in a boat.'

EATING À LA CARTE

As well as the first-class dining room, there was an exclusive à la carte restaurant on board known as the Ritz. It was run by a man named Luigi Gatti, who had previously managed London's prestigious Oddenino's restaurant, and was staffed by waiters who were predominantly French and Italian. Eating in the Ritz was an expensive optional extra, not covered by the price of the ticket, but it was fully booked for the *Titanic*'s entire voyage. The food was sumptuous and every whim of the customers could be catered for by the team of 68 staff, including separate cooks for the soup, fish, pastry, roasts and entrées. There was a wine butler, a maître d', an iceman, a glassman, carvers, platemen and page boys to do any running about the customers might require. Situated on B Deck, near the most expensive suites, this lavish restaurant was reserved for the wealthiest of the ship's clientèle.

"BE BRITISH": The Last Words of the "Titanic's" Captain.

COMMANDER EDWARD J. SMITH, R.N.R.

Born in the Year 1853   Died April 15, 1912

ABOVE
White Star Line had such confidence in Captain Smith that they put him at the helm whenever there was a maiden voyage.

He turned to Eloise, took her face in his hands and spoke seriously. 'I never expected to ask you to obey, but this is one time you must. It is only a matter of form to have women and children first. The boat is thoroughly equipped, and everyone on her will be saved.'

'Are you being absolutely honest?' she asked.

'Yes.'

At that, she felt somewhat reassured. He kissed her good-bye, then helped her climb into the boat. As it was being lowered, he shouted to her from the deck, 'Keep your hands in your pockets. It is very cold weather.'

It was the last time Eloise would see Lucian.

LEARNING OF HER WIDOWHOOD

Eloise kept her eyes glued to the deck of the ship as Lifeboat 4 was rowed away. She only saw one more boat being launched from the port side, but a neighbour reassured her that men were being loaded on the starboard side. She hoped desperately that someone would have directed Lucian over there.

A few people thought they saw a light on the horizon and speculated that it could be another rescue ship, so they rowed towards it. Eloise's eyes remained on the *Titanic* as its bow slid lower and lower into the water, then finally tipped up on end before disappearing. They all heard the cries for help but they were too far away to return. It didn't occur to Eloise for a moment that her husband might be among them. She had believed him when he said there were enough boats for all. She assumed those crying out were third-class passengers who had overslept and hadn't got up on deck in time. She also felt sorry for Captain Smith, because she'd heard it said that captains should always go down with their ship.

It was bitterly cold. The stars overhead were bright and the sea was calm. As dawn broke, they saw the sparkle of icebergs around them and, finally, the reassuring shape of the *Carpathia*. By the time they drew up alongside her and were hauled on board, the sea was starting to get choppy.

Eloise wanted to start searching for Lucian right away, but the ship's doctor advised her to find a place to rest and said that he would find her, because they were taking a roll call. She saw Bruce Ismay, director of the White Star shipping line, come aboard and heard him demand a private room, which she thought bad manners, considering some first-class ladies were having to curl up and sleep on the floor of the public rooms. A kind lady offered Eloise her own berth and she went to lie down but couldn't sleep. She couldn't help wondering why Lucian hadn't come to find her yet. Where was he?

BELOW
Some claimed to have seen Captain Smith in the water after the sinking, but said that he refused all offers of rescue.

WHEN THE TITANIC WENT DOWN : THE LAST OF CAPTAIN SMITH

J. BRUCE ISMAY

The White Star Line was a family business, founded by Bruce Ismay's father. Bruce had taken over as chairman in 1899. He commissioned several new ships to keep the firm at the forefront of the transatlantic trade, and was so proud of the *Titanic* that he decided to travel on the maiden voyage, in one of her best suites. Some claim he urged the ship's engineers to push her to maximum speed, but it's unlikely he would have had any say in this, and he certainly denied it. After the collision, Ismay helped to load passengers onto lifeboats and then, just before it was lowered, he stepped into Collapsible C. Newspapers called him 'J. Brute Ismay' for saving himself while women and children remained on board. Eloise Smith criticized him fiercely in the press for his high-handed attitude on the *Carpathia*. 'I'm Ismay, I'm Ismay, get me a stateroom,' she quoted him demanding. Afterwards, he was ostracized by society and stayed out of the public eye for the rest of his life.

RIGHT
J. Bruce Ismay

The ship was very crowded, with men sleeping on the engine room floor and anywhere they could find a space, but within a few hours, Eloise started to panic. If Lucian was on board, surely he would have found her by now? He would have searched everywhere until he tracked her down. She talked to other survivors and learned that there hadn't been enough lifeboats for all the passengers. In fact, hers had been one of the last to leave the ship. Lucian's chances of survival after its launch were remote. Eloise concluded that he'd known that and had lied to save her life, because if she'd known the truth she simply would never have gone without him. She broke down at the realization that she was in all likelihood a widow.

Fury took root alongside her overwhelming grief when she heard that Mr Ismay was in the best room on the *Carpathia*, with a sign on the door that read 'Please do not knock.' Eloise found it unbearable that he had escaped when her husband had not.

Later that day, there was a knock on the door of her cabin, and Eloise found a gentleman standing outside wearing an ill-fitting suit. He introduced himself as Robert Daniel, a banker from Virginia, and explained that he had come to offer her his protection as she was the only unaccompanied Southern woman on board the ship.

She asked how he had escaped the sinking ship and he told her that as the *Titanic* went down, he had leaped into the water and thrashed around madly until he reached a lifeboat. He was wearing only his woollen nightwear and so was extremely

lucky to have survived. A *Carpathia* passenger had donated the suit he was wearing.

Eloise asked if she could borrow money from him to send a Marconi-gram to her family and Lucian's, knowing how worried they would be. In the wireless room the operator told her she didn't need to pay, but she insisted, thinking it might get her wire on the top of the pile. In fact, it was never sent, and their families only heard the news of her survival and Lucian's demise when the whole list of survivors was cabled through on Tuesday, 16th April. Over a hundred messages were not sent because the operators were simply overloaded.

It took three-and-a-half days for the *Carpathia* to reach New York. In the meantime, Eloise was consoled by Robert Daniel. When they docked, he carefully led her down the gangplank on his arm and looked after her until he was able to hand her to her father, Congressman Hughes.

'THE WHITE WIDOW'

Eloise returned to Huntington by train, accompanied by her father. A thousand people had turned out to gawp as the

ABOVE
The Carpathia *docked at New York's Pier 54, where police had roped off an area in which survivors could greet relatives without being photographed by the hordes of press reporters.*

VIKING PRINCESS

On 8th April 1966, almost fifty-four years to the day after Lucian Smith perished on the *Titanic*, his son was nearing the end of a week's Caribbean cruise on the *Viking Princess* with his wife and children. In the early hours of the morning, a fire broke out. The passengers were summoned on deck, and Lucian Jr's blood chilled when he heard the shout, 'Women and children to the lifeboats'. Would history repeat itself? Did he face the same fate as his father? In fact, the experienced crew of the *Princess* got everyone into their life-jackets and lowered into boats within minutes. Nearby freighters picked them up and transported them to Guantanamo Bay in Cuba. All survived apart from two passengers, who suffered heart attacks. None of them got wet. The safety legislation passed after the sinking of the *Titanic* had helped avoid another disaster, and had saved the lives of Lucian and Eloise Smith's descendants.

Titanic survivor arrived at Huntington station, and the police had to be called to escort them to her grandmother's house. There she was able to mourn in peace.

On 12th May, Eloise attended a memorial service for her husband at the same church in which they had been married only three months earlier. On 20th May, she was called to testify at the Senate Inquiry into the ship's sinking and, ever the politician's daughter, she acquitted herself calmly and with great dignity, describing step by step what had happened to her and Lucian on that dreadful night. She wore a white dress and the press dubbed her 'the white widow', but there was no doubting the depths of her grief. She wasn't seen in public again until the following year, by which time she was mother to a little boy, whom she called Lucian Smith Junior.

Congressman Hughes felt strongly that at least part of the Smith family mining fortune should be settled on Lucian Jr and, when a financial offer for child support was not forthcoming, he and Eloise instituted legal action. It eventually came to nothing, however, as it transpired that none of the family money had been in Lucian's name. He had lived on a stipend of $500 a month.

During 1913, Robert Daniel frequently came to call on Eloise, and it was comforting for her to be able to talk to someone who had been through the same experience. Their friendship turned to romance and, just before her baby son's first birthday, they announced to family and close friends that they planned to wed. Her father was against the match at first, not least because it might jeopardize the outcome of their ongoing lawsuit against the Smiths. Though, eventually, he gave his permission, and the wedding took place in New York on 18th August 1914. Immediately afterwards, Robert had to travel to Europe on business and was stuck there for two months due to the start of World War I, because all of the ships were fully booked by Americans trying to escape the fighting. It was the end of October before they were able to move into a home together in Philadelphia, where Robert took on the role of Lucian Jr's father.

The marriage wasn't to last. Perhaps Eloise had jumped into it too quickly, looking for distraction from the awful weight of her grief and clinging to the man who had comforted her through the first agonizing days after the sinking. They separated in 1918 and finally divorced in 1923, after Eloise found out that he was living with a blonde woman in New York.

Eloise was to marry twice more but neither marriage lasted, and on her divorce from her fourth husband she reverted to the name Smith. It was the name by which her adored son was known, and the name of the man who had been the love of her life. Her granddaughter, Cathy Gay, told a reporter from the *Huntington Quarterly*, 'She never completely recovered emotionally from Lucian's death or from witnessing the tragic deaths of the other people on that ship.' Eloise died of a heart attack at the age of just forty-six. Cathy said she died of a broken heart.

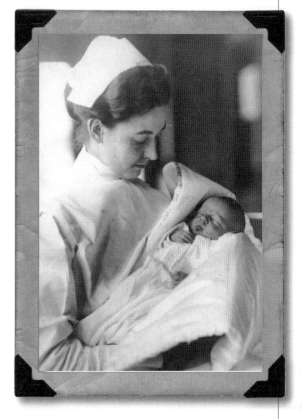

ABOVE
Lucian Smith Jr in the arms of a nurse. After his birth, Madeleine Astor, who had also been pregnant on the Titanic, *sent Eloise a telegram of congratulations.*

> *'She never completely recovered emotionally from Lucian's death or from witnessing the tragic deaths of the other people on that ship.'*

PASSENGER MANIFEST

1ST CLASS

Name, *John Pillsbury Snyder (b. 8th January 1888).*

Name, *Nelle Stevenson (b. 15th January 1889).*

Married, *22nd January 1912.*

Point of embarkation, *Southampton.*

Ticket no. *21228.*   Suite, *B45.*

DECK B (PROMENADE DECK.)

SUITE ROOMS

3 3 3 1 3 1 1 1 3 3 3 3

B.90 B.88 B.84 B.82 B.78 B.76 B.72 B.70 B.66 B.64 B.60 B.58

1 1 3 1 1 1 3 1 1 1 1 1

WARDROBE ROOM WARDROBE ROOM WARDROBE ROOM WARDROBE ROOM WARDROBE ROOM WARDROBE ROOM WARDROBE ROOM WARDROBE ROOM WARDROBE ROOM WARDROBE ROOM WARDROBE ROOM

B.92 B.86 B.80 B.74 B.68 B.62

GENTS LAVT.

BATH B 100 3 BATH 3 B 102 BATH STEWARDESS

BATH 1 2 W 1 2 BATH LADIES LAVT.

BATH B.99 B 101

3 3

B.91 B.85 B.79 B.73 B.67 B.61

WARDROBE ROOM WARDROBE ROOM WARDROBE ROOM WARDROBE ROOM WARDROBE ROOM WARDROBE ROOM WARDROBE ROOM WARDROBE ROOM WARDROBE ROOM WARDROBE ROOM

1 1 3 1 1 1 1 1 1 1

B.89 B.87 B.83 B.81 B.77 B.75 B.71 B.69 B.65 B.63 B.59 B.57

3 3 3 3 3 3 3 3 3 3 3

SUITE ROOMS

ROOMS B 53, 54, 55, 56, 57, 58, 59, 60, 63, 64, 65, 66, 69, 70, 71, 72, 75, 76, 77, 78, 81, 82, 83, 84, 87, 88, 89, 90 ARE

OPPOSITE

The first page of a letter sent by a Titanic passenger to her fiancé. The writer says that the luxury liner is like 'the Savoy afloat' and asks that they book a cabin for their honeymoon.

John & Nelle
Snyder

Many transatlantic passengers sought out ships on which Edward Smith was captain, because of his long record of reliable service and his congenial manner. Nelle Snyder was horrified, however, when she found out he would be captain of the *Titanic*, mistaking him for another Captain Smith who had been in charge of their honeymoon voyage to Europe.

THIS PAGE *John and Nelle came from wealthy families, and looked forward to having children of their own.*

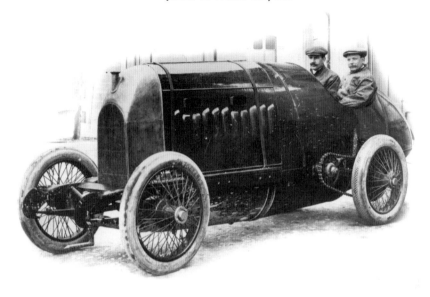

ABOVE
The Fiat S76 was built for speed, but Fords remained America's most popular car for some time to come.

JOHN PILLSBURY SNYDER was a great catch. He came from one of Minneapolis's oldest families, with solid roots in the worlds of commerce and politics. John's grandfather had been Governor of Minnesota from 1876 to 1882, his great-uncle founded the Pillsbury flour company, and his father was a prominent lawyer who served as President of the Board of Regents for the University of Minnesota. John studied at that university, where he was known as a talented athlete. Later, in 1911, he turned his attention to the burgeoning automobile industry.

This was the era in which automobiles in the United States were graduating from toys for wealthy amateur enthusiasts to a means of transport for better-off families. The Model T Ford, introduced in 1908, was the first car that upper-middle-class families could afford, costing $850, only slightly more than the rate per person for the most expensive suite on the *Titanic*. John Snyder wasn't the first to see that cars were going to become more popular in the future, but he made a wise move in December 1911 when he opened the Snyder Garage on South Tenth Street, Minneapolis. He sold cars from there and also ran a truck dealership.

A month after opening the garage, he married Nelle Snyder, an attractive girl from a wealthy Minneapolis family, and they set off to Europe on a three-month honeymoon. The trip began inauspiciously, when Captain Smith gave his orders to sail full steam ahead while the ship was still tied to the pier in

> *'Can't we change ships?' she begged John.*
> *'I don't think this man is careful enough.'*

New York. According to Nelle, they nearly took the whole structure with them. Later, the ship ran onto a sandbar off Gibraltar and had to wait for the tide, so they were unable to go ashore. The couple were glad to leave the ship at Naples, fearing there would be another mishap.

They travelled up through Italy, seeing all the sights of Rome, Florence and Venice, and John had some business meetings with representatives of the Fiat car firm to explore whether it would be worth stocking Fiats at his garage back home. They took a train across France and a ferry across the English Channel to London, where they did some shopping and John refilled his humidor at his favourite cigar merchant.

They had been booked to sail on another ship home from Southampton, but it was cancelled because of a coal workers' strike, and they heard they were being transferred onto the *Titanic*. At first, Nelle was very pleased. They had seen the advertisements for 'The Greatest Ship in the World' and looked forward to sailing on its maiden voyage. However, the night before the departure, she discovered that they would be sailing under Captain E. J. Smith, and jumped to the erroneous conclusion that it was the same man who had captained them on the way over from the United States.

'Can't we change ships?' she begged John. 'I don't think this man is careful enough.'

John told her not to worry, that the *Titanic* was unsinkable. Everyone said so. Besides, after three months' absence, he needed to get home to his garage business as soon as possible.

Nelle's fears must have multiplied when the *Titanic* manoeuvred out of dock in Southampton. Its wash tore another ship, the *New York*, free of its moorings and she drifted into the *Titanic*'s path. It was only the speedy actions of Captain Smith, who ordered the engines to be put into reverse, that prevented a collision.

ON BOARD THE *TITANIC*

The Snyders' stateroom on B Deck was on the starboard side, close to the millionaires' suite occupied by the Cardeza family (whose money was made from Kentucky blue jeans) and just along from the suite of Helen and Dickinson Bishop, another honeymoon couple. Theirs was a sumptuous room, with a curtained-off, full-size bed, a small table with a reading lamp and chairs and ornate wood panelling on the walls.

John and Nelle soon made friends with the Bishops and, through them, were introduced to the Astors and the Harders. The four honeymooning couples often socialized together in the first-class lounge. After their intensive sightseeing in the great European capital cities, it was a leisurely pace of life. They played cards, read and wrote postcards home, and John

LEFT
If their husbands retired to the smoking room after dinner, the women could congregate in the cosy reading room to chat among themselves.

THE PRICE OF SUITES AND CABINS

In general, the higher the deck, the more expensive the accommodation. Prices also varied according to the number of people in the party and the amenities in the rooms.

Modern price equivalents are given in parentheses.

The Cardezas' grand suite with private promenade on B Deck cost £945 (£53,156/$94,500).

On B Deck, a suite of rooms for one or two people, comprising three bed/sitting rooms, two wardrobe rooms, a private bathroom and lavatory and a separate servants' room cost £304 (£17,100/$30,400).

On C Deck, John Jacob Astor paid £247 10 shillings and sixpence (£13,923/$24,700) for a similar suite.

A smaller B Deck suite with wardrobe room, private bathroom and lavatory cost £155 (£8,718/$15,500), and without a private bathroom £110 (£6,188/$11,000).

A similar C Deck suite cost £10 less – £145 (£8,156/$14,500) with private bathroom and £100 (£5,625/$10,000) without.

First-class staterooms for two on B and C Decks ranged from £57 (£3,206/$5,700) to £91 (£5,119/$9,100).

A second-class cabin for two was £26 (£1,462/$2,600).

A superior third-class cabin for two was £16 2 shillings (£905/$1,610).

A basic third-class cabin for two was £7 15 shillings (£436/$775).

and Nelle often talked about the house they would like to buy back in Minneapolis. After dinner, John usually joined the men to smoke a cigar in the smoking room, perhaps with a brandy or two on the side.

On the evening of Sunday, 14th April, the Snyders were already in bed when the ship collided with the iceberg. John went out to see what was going on and was advised by their steward that they should dress and make their way up to the boat deck. There they found their new friends the Astors and the Bishops standing in a huddle, and they saw sailors stripping the covers off the lifeboats. Everyone was asking what had happened and wondering what they should do.

Seeing Captain Smith coming down from the bridge, John Jacob Astor approached to ask his guidance. He returned with the news that women and children were to be lowered in the lifeboats and that they should all put on their life-jackets.

As John and Nelle walked down to their room, Nelle insisted that she wasn't going to get into one of those tiny boats and be lowered goodness knows how far down to the dark, freezing ocean. 'I'd rather stay on the ship,' she said. 'Nothing's going to happen to it, after all.'

John agreed that it seemed very unlikely, but said they should do as the captain instructed and return to the boat deck with their life-jackets. He made Nelle put on her fur coat against the cold.

Back on the boat deck, they couldn't see the Astors, but they rejoined the Bishops. All were in agreement that they would rather stay on the ship even though they could now feel that it was listing somewhat. Lifeboat 7 was swung out and the crew called out that they should get on board. Still John and Nelle hung back.

'Please, will you brides and grooms set an example by getting on the boat?' begged a crewman.

The Bishops boarded and, according to Nelle, a crewman grabbed her arm, pulled her toward the lifeboat and 'literally threw' her in. By this time, there was quite a gap between the boat and the edge of the ship due to the list. John followed right behind and they sat down near the Bishops.

When the boat was lowered at 12.45am, they realized the only crew on board were two young boys, who admitted they

OPPOSITE
A private promenade in one of the two millionaires' suites on B Deck.

had never been in one of the lifeboats before. As they reached the ocean surface, icy water began to flood in because the plug in the bottom of the boat was not in place. John, who had some knowledge of boating from frequent sailing trips back home on Lake Minnetonka, helped to replace it.

The head count they took came to 28. The capacity of the lifeboat was 65, but no one thought anything of it.

THE LONGEST HOURS OF THEIR LIVES

John was a big, strapping man and throughout the night he helped to row Lifeboat 7. They went about 200 yards away from the ship, then stopped, reluctant to go further from what was still seen as the safety of its huge bulk. However, as they watched, it was obvious that the bow was lowering further and further into the water. Despite the evidence of their own eyes, John and Nelle still refused to believe it would sink, until they heard two sharp explosions, which they thought must be the boilers blowing up as water rushed into the boiler room. Other people who reported these sounds thought the boilers had come loose from their casings and crashed down into the bow once the ship tipped.

According to John, 'The *Titanic* was torn in two. For a moment the great masses of steel and iron poised in the air. Then slowly they sank and a few minutes later there was nothing but wreckage on the surface.'

Nelle later told her grandchildren, 'The ship hardly made a sound. It slipped into the sea like a big fish.'

They saw passengers being tossed into the water and struggling for their lives in the freezing temperatures. Their cries gradually died out. Despite the fact that Lifeboat 7 was less than half full, and not as far from the scene as other boats, no one suggested that they should turn back to help. Each sat, thinking their own thoughts, thanking God that it wasn't them in the water. Lifeboat 5, although it wasn't full either, drew up alongside and transferred some of their passengers across to even up the numbers.

They searched in vain for a lantern and some food and water. It later transpired that, in fact, there were crackers and water inside compartments in the bow. Meanwhile, Helen Bishop lifted Nelle's spirits by relating the prophecy made by

OPPOSITE
Captain Edward Smith in Southampton with his Irish wolfhound, shortly before the Titanic *sailed.*

CAPTAIN E. J. SMITH

The *Titanic*'s maiden voyage was to have been the last of Edward Smith's long and illustrious career, during which he captained seven ships owned by the White Star Line. He intended to retire and spend more time with his wife and daughter in Southampton. For someone of his experience, the *Titanic*'s run to New York should have been straightforward, and he probably felt relaxed about it. Too relaxed, according to the US Senate Inquiry into the sinking. Why didn't he order the ship to slow down after receiving warnings of ice earlier on Sunday, 14th April? After the collision, why didn't he make sure the evacuation into the lifeboats was carried out efficiently, with each boat filled to capacity? Some reports suggest that he committed suicide on the bridge as the ship sank, while others claim to have seen him swimming in the water. What's certain is that he didn't survive to tell his story.

a fortune-teller while they were in Cairo. According to this fortune-teller, Helen was to survive a shipwreck and then an earthquake before dying in a car accident. In the circumstances, Nelle was much heartened.

At 4am, they heard the cry, 'A ship!' and saw the rockets fired by the *Carpathia* to announce her arrival. They turned and rowed towards it. As dawn broke, they saw they were part of a tiny flotilla of rowing boats making their way towards the ship, surrounded by icebergs on all sides.

LIFE GOES ON

The Snyders appear to have recovered from their ordeal more successfully than many other survivors. Shortly after their safe return, they moved into a sprawling, shingle-style house on Lookout Point in Minneapolis, on the shores of Lake Minnetonka. John's automobile business grew ever more successful and he also became vice president of Millers & Traders State Bank. He served in World War I and acquitted himself honourably, which must have gone some way to assuaging any survivor guilt he may have felt. They had three children, a girl and two boys, who provided them with grandchildren in due course.

John and Nelle travelled to Europe only once more, in 1939, and while they were there World War II broke out. They had to cut short their trip or else risk being stranded. It seemed their trips across the Atlantic were doomed and, from then on, they resolved to stay at home in the United States.

The Snyders appear to have recovered from their ordeal more successfully than many other survivors.

THE LIFEBOATS

The 14 standard lifeboats on the *Titanic* had a capacity of 65 people each. Lifeboats 1 and 2 were both designed for 40 people and the collapsibles A, B, C and D each had a capacity of 47. It should have been possible to rescue 1,178 people in these boats, yet only 711 survived. Officer Lightoller later testified that he didn't like to fill the boats to capacity while they were still suspended from the davits in case they couldn't take the strain, but he expected more would board once they were launched. In fact, only two lifeboats and two collapsibles picked up survivors from the water. Lifeboat 14, under the command of Fifth Officer Harold Lowe, rescued four people, one of whom later died. Lifeboat 4, commanded by Quartermaster Walter Perkis, picked up eight crewmen, two of whom later died. Collapsible A was washed off the ship as it sank and was partly flooded. Of the 20 on board, only 12 survived. Collapsible B overturned as it was launched but about 30 people, including Second Officer Lightoller, managed to balance on its base; 27 of them remained alive by morning.

PASSENGER MANIFEST

2ND

CLASS

Name, ... *Edward Beane (b. 19th November 1879).*

Name, ... *Ethel Clarke (b. 15th November 1892).*

Married, ... *March 1912.*

Point of embarkation, ... *Southampton.*

Ticket no. .... *2908.*

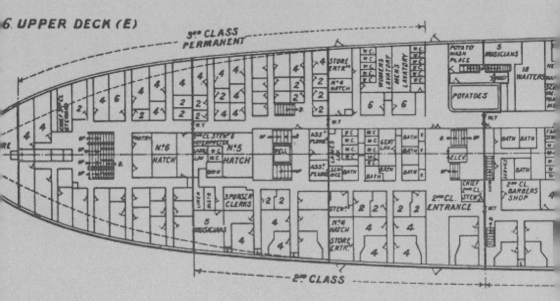

6. UPPER DECK (E)

OPPOSITE
*A banknote rescued
from the* Titanic.
*Many lost savings
they had entrusted
to the ship's purser.*

— 142 —

Edward & Ethel Beane

'I swam for hours before being rescued,' Edward Beane told a reporter. It may have felt like that but, in fact, few men could have survived for longer than 20 minutes in a water temperature of 28 degrees Fahrenheit – four degrees below freezing.

BY APRIL 1912, Edward Beane had already crossed the Atlantic several times, at least once on the *Lusitania*, whose maiden voyage was in 1907. One of ten children born to George and Mary Beane in a small village outside Norwich, on leaving school Edward had gone into the construction industry, finding work as a manual labourer. It was a job without prospects or decent pay and, in 1906, along with two of his brothers, he decided to try to make his fortune in the New World.

She was only fourteen to his twenty-seven, but she liked the idea of emigrating ...

Before he left Norfolk, Edward asked Ethel Clarke, the daughter of a colleague of his father's, if she would do him the honour of becoming his bride once he had raised enough money to set up a home for them. She was only fourteen to his twenty-seven, but she liked the idea of emigrating and making a better life for the children they would one day have, so for the next six years she waited for Edward. She worked as a hotel chambermaid and used her earnings to create a trousseau of hand-embroidered linens and household necessities that she could take with her to America.

OPPOSITE
Edward and Ethel Beane, photographed in 1931, when they spoke to a reporter about their experiences.

BELOW *The construction industry paid poorly, so many labourers chose to emigrate to the 'Land of Opportunity' to seek their fortune.*

THE *LUSITANIA*

Smaller and faster than the *Titanic*, the *Lusitania* and her sister ship the *Mauretania* were seen as the height of luxury at their launch. The *Lusitania* was said to have particularly comfortable third-class compartments. Its design included fewer watertight bulkheads than the *Titanic*, however, and this difference would be tragically counterpointed. When the *Lusitania* was holed by a torpedo from a German U-boat in May 1915, it sank in 18 minutes, whereas the *Titanic*'s design kept her afloat for 2 hours and 40 minutes after hitting the iceberg. Although there were more than enough lifeboats on the *Lusitania* for everyone, the ship was soon listing so badly that only six could be launched. Of the 1,959 people on board, 1,198 died.

It was difficult for Ethel to wait patiently. If there was ever a longer-than-usual gap between his letters, she worried that her fiancé's head had been turned by some pretty girl in New York. When he came back to visit, travelling steerage to save money, Edward reassured her by reporting the wages he was earning as a bricklayer – much better than he could have made in England – and with stories about the little house he was hoping to rent for them once she joined him.

At last, they felt they had enough money – $500 in savings and £26 to pay for a second-class ticket on the *Titanic*'s maiden voyage. They were married in Norwich and said goodbye to their families and friends before setting off for Southampton.

SECOND-CLASS ACCOMMODATION

Edward and Ethel may not have been able to enjoy the much-publicized amenities open to first-class passengers, such as the Turkish baths and the gymnasium, but the public rooms in second class were more plush than those on most first-class liners of the day.

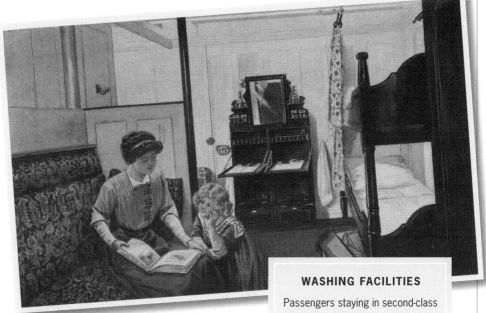

There was oak panelling in the dining room and smoking room, a well-stocked sycamore-lined library, mahogany furniture upholstered in red or green leather, thick red or green carpets underfoot and an outdoor promenade from which to gaze out at the ocean while stretching your legs or relaxing in a deckchair.

Second-class passengers could pass their days listening to concerts given by one of the ship's two bands, playing cards, reading or taking part in games of quoits on deck, until summoned to the dining room for their meals: breakfast from 8.30 to 10.30am, luncheon from 1 to 2.30pm and dinner from 6pm. On the morning of Sunday, 14th April, Edward and Ethel chose to attend a church service in the first-class dining saloon led by Captain Smith, with Wallace Hartley's quintet accompanying the hymns. After evening dinner, there was hymn singing in the second-class dining room, attended by more than a hundred passengers, which continued until 10pm.

WASHING FACILITIES

Passengers staying in second-class cabins didn't have their own private bathrooms; instead, they had a washbasin attached to the wall, which could be folded down for use. When you pressed a lever, cold water spouted out of a tap leading from a metal tank situated in the wall behind a mirror. Hot water was brought around in pitchers by the stewards. Waste water drained into a canister down by the floor, and when you had finished using the basin, it could be folded back up to the wall to save space. The steward for each corridor was responsible for filling up the water tanks and disposing of the waste water. Of course, in first class, passengers had the luxury of hot and cold running water in their private bathrooms.

PREVIOUS PAGE
(BOTTOM)
The Lusitania.

(TOP)
*The furnishings and
decor in second-class
cabins were perhaps a
couple of years behind
the times, but smarter
than would be found
in even the first-class
accommodations on
other ships.*

Edward and Ethel were in their cabin at the time of the collision. They thought nothing of the slight jolt until a woman in the cabin next to theirs knocked on their door.

'We've hit something,' she told them with panic in her voice. 'Hurry! The ship is in danger.'

'Don't worry,' Edward reassured Ethel. 'It's probably a drill. They do that on ships from time to time as a precaution.' He was the one with experience of transatlantic travel, so she believed him.

It was only when their neighbour banged on the door for the second time, saying that they had been ordered to go on deck immediately wearing warm clothes and bringing their life-jackets, that they became alarmed.

'Should I pack our things?' Ethel wondered, looking at her few pieces of jewellery and her beautiful linens.

Edward thought they shouldn't delay. 'We'd better go up and see what's happening,' he said. 'There's something not quite right about this.'

ESCAPE FROM THE SINKING SHIP

There are several different versions of what happened to Edward and Ethel Beane after they made their way up to the starboard boat deck.

'Women and children first,' was the cry, and Ethel Beane was ushered onto Lifeboat 13, with time for only a quick, desperate kiss for her new husband. The crew began to lower the boat at 1.25am and the occupants shouted a warning as it narrowly avoided a discharge pipe gushing out water. They stopped briefly and a crewman, looking down, realized there were still spaces on board.

'Are there no more women and children here?' he asked.

A second-class passenger named Lawrence Beesley confirmed that was the case, and the crewman told him to jump on board and take a place, which he did. A couple more women got on at the same time and the boat was lowered to the water, where it narrowly avoided a collision with Lifeboat 15. The crewmen rowed out to about a mile from the ship, worried that, if it sank, they could be pulled under by the suction.

Ethel strained her eyes to try to catch sight of Edward, whom she had last seen standing on deck, waving at her.

OPPOSITE
The lights on the Titanic
*stayed on until moments
before she sank.*

If Edward was guilty of embroidering the story of his rescue slightly, he would have been by no means unique among male Titanic survivors.

Surely, she thought, he must get on one of the other boats. She could hear the incongruous strains of the band playing on deck. Then she watched in horror as the *Titanic* tipped up on end and slid slowly under the black surface of the water, creating hardly a ripple. She later described hearing the 'anguished cries of those on board, which was like one great human wail'. No one who heard that sound ever forgot it.

Immediately after the ship sank, there were distraught calls from the men in the water: 'Over here!' 'Please help me!' 'God save me!' One of the passengers on Lifeboat 13 asked the officer in charge shouldn't they go back to pick up survivors, because they weren't full. He refused, saying that they risked being overrun, which would sink the lifeboat and kill them all. From other boats, Ethel thought she could hear guns being fired to stop people from attempting to board. All the time her heart was fit to bursting as she worried about what was happening to her husband.

THE FATE OF EDWARD BEANE

Edward and Ethel later told two different versions of the story of their reunion.

According to one, Edward kept his eyes on his wife's lifeboat and, as the *Titanic* went down, jumped into the water and swam with all his strength until he reached Lifeboat 13. If the lifeboat had been a mile away from the ship, and he was able to survive in the freezing water for the maximum 20 minutes, this story is just feasible. According to this account, a crewman on the lifeboat, seeing a swimmer approach, gave the instruction to pull him up – no mean feat in itself. When Ethel made out his face in the darkness, she cried out in delight and shock, 'My husband! My God, it's Ted.'

Having made this superhuman effort to be reunited with his young bride, Edward would have been trembling violently, semi-conscious and unable to speak for some time. One problem with the story is that Lawrence Beesley, a passenger on the same lifeboat who published a memoir shortly afterwards, made no mention of the rescue of a swimmer from the water. It was an event you would expect to merit at least a passing note.

The Beanes also told a journalist a different version, in which Edward was picked up from the water by another lifeboat, not his wife's. They claimed that they failed to find each other on board the *Carpathia* and were only reunited when it docked in New York. If this is the true story, we can only imagine the despair they felt as they searched the decks and salons of the *Carpathia*, asking anyone who would listen for help, and the euphoria on their final reunion. However, this version also seems unlikely, because one of the roll calls on board the *Carpathia* would surely have alerted each of them to the other's presence.

Another possibility is that Edward Beane boarded Lifeboat 13 at around the same time as Lawrence Beesley, at the point when women had stopped coming forward and the crew allowed some men to get on. It seemed that crew on the starboard side of the ship were far more lenient in their application of the 'women and children' rule. If this were the case, then Edward didn't even get his feet wet, which raises the question why he would invent a story and tell a journalist in 1931 that he 'swam for hours'. Perhaps he suffered from the common reaction of 'male survivor guilt'. Why had any men survived the sinking of the *Titanic* when there were women and children who did not? They would not want to admit

HYPOTHERMIA

As the core body temperature drops, the muscles tense and shiver, making it harder to control movement, while blood pressure and breathing rates decrease. The life-jackets worn by *Titanic* passengers and crew would have provided a layer of insulation and helped to keep the upper part of their bodies out of the water, but they were cumbersome objects and would have severely restricted swimming, making Edward's story of a mile-long swim even more unlikely. As their body temperatures dropped dangerously low, those passengers in the water would have become semi-conscious and may have acted irrationally, perhaps even resisting attempts to be rescued. Death would have resulted from heart or respiratory failure. The length of time this took would have depended on many factors: amount of body fat, age and layers of insulation in the form of clothing. It is thought that just over fifty *Titanic* passengers were rescued from the water, but around one-fifth of them died before they could reach the *Carpathia*. Charles Joughin, the *Titanic*'s chief banker, claimed he spent two-and-a-half hours in the water and speculated that the glass of whiskey he had drunk helped to ward off the cold.

THE RELIEF EFFORT

Mrs Nelson Henry, the wife of a New York port official, was instrumental in organizing the Women's Relief Committee to raise funds and offer practical help to *Titanic* survivors. So efficient were they that by Friday, 19th April, they had raised more money than they needed. They weren't the only ones helping. The Red Cross were on hand at the port and the Municipal Lodging House on East 25th Street threw open its doors and agreed to provide food and board for anybody that needed it. When the *Carpathia* docked, there were 20 ambulances on standby to ferry survivors to hospital, and St Vincent's hospital in Greenwich Village set aside 120 beds. New York's immigrant communities – the Germans, Irish, Italians, Swedish and Jews – all prepared to help their own, while Mrs William K. Vanderbilt called all her friends and managed to arrange 100 automobiles to pick up survivors from the port and take them wherever they needed to go.

BELOW *A baggage coupon that could never be redeemed.*

that they had ignored the Edwardian principle of chivalry. If Edward was indeed guilty of embroidering the story of his rescue slightly, he would have been by no means unique among male *Titanic* survivors.

MAKING A NEW LIFE

Edward and Ethel Beane walked out of the port in New York utterly destitute, having lost their clothes, Ethel's trousseau and their life savings. They wandered into the Chelsea Hotel, where they were discovered by Mrs George F. Stott, a volunteer working for the Women's Relief Committee, which had been set up to help survivors.

'You poor things,' she cried, and set about finding them a change of clothes and enough money for their train fare to Rochester, where Edward had work waiting for him. She also took Edward down to the White Star Line to file his claim for compensation.

They had entrusted $300 cash to the ship's purser, and Edward was aghast when he was asked to produce the receipt as proof.

'It went down with the ship!' he cried. 'Like everything else I own.'

He was told he could have $20 there and then, providing he signed a form waiving any further claim.

Mrs Stott insisted that he do no such thing, but instead fight for proper compensation for everything he had lost. Unfortunately, in those days, there was no automatic right

ABOVE
*Crowds of anxious
relatives descended on
the White Star Line
offices in New York,
desperate for news.*

of redress. The White Star Line refused to reimburse any
passengers for the cost of their fare, claiming that they had
been transported to New York as promised. Each passenger
had to submit a claim for loss of life, injury and the value of
the goods they had lost for scrutiny by loss adjusters before
a figure could be decided. A US commission set a maximum
compensation fund value of $97,772.02, but the total passenger
claims filed came to more than $16 million. Each claim
judged valid was apportioned a payment on a pro rata basis
according to the available funds. This, of course, took time: the
money didn't reach claimants until the second half of 1916.

By that time, Edward and Ethel were living in Rochester,
where they stayed for the rest of their lives. They both vowed
never to set foot on a ship again. They gave an interview to a
local Rochester paper in 1931, then vowed never again to talk
about what had happened that night, except to close family.
It was a memory they wanted to put behind them forever.

PASSENGER MANIFEST

2ND CLASS

Name, ... *John Chapman (b. 1875).*

Name, ... *Sarah Elizabeth (Lizzie) Lawry (b.1883).*

Married, ... *26th December 1911.*

Point of embarkation, ... *Southampton.*

Ticket no. .... *29037.*

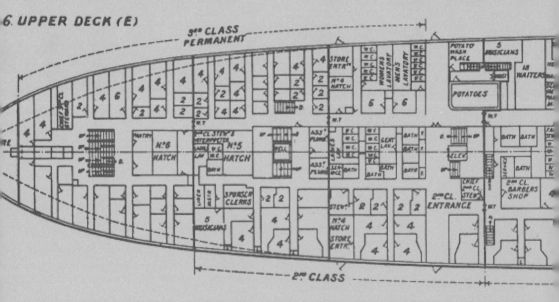

OPPOSITE

The pocket watch of John Chapman. The watch stopped at the moment the couple lost their lives together.

John & Lizzie
Chapman

Some women refused to get into the lifeboats because they seemed so fragile as they dangled precariously above the dark ocean. Some didn't take the danger seriously until it was too late. Many other women, including Lizzie Chapman, simply refused to leave their beloved husbands' sides.

J OHN CHAPMAN'S FAMILY lived in St Neot, a small market town in central Cornwall, surrounded by farms and moorland. If you didn't want a life spent farming, there wasn't much else you could do there to earn a living. John's father was a tenant farmer with five children, of whom John was the youngest, and it was simply assumed that John would help on the farm as soon as he left school.

John toiled alongside his father for 18 years, during which time relations became increasingly strained and there were frequent shouting matches. It wasn't an easy life. Their profits were dependent on the market price of milk and cattle feed, as well as the vagaries of the Cornish climate. John wanted to save enough to marry his sweetheart, Lizzie Lawry, but by the age of thirty-one he didn't have anything like the amount needed to pay the deposit on a small farm of his own – and besides, he was tired of the farming lifestyle. In 1906, he decided to emigrate to Canada and find a way of earning a living there before coming back to fetch the girl he loved.

Lizzie wrote to John every week and waited eagerly for his replies. He spent four years in Canada, then moved to Spokane, Washington, where he lived with his cousin, Andrew Wilton, and got work as a grave digger at Fairmount Cemetery. Lizzie's parents were dead, so she stayed with her aunt, Emma Lawry, and helped to look after her extended family while waiting for John's return.

At last, in the winter of 1911, John came back to Cornwall for six months and he and Lizzie were married at the Wesleyan Chapel in Liskeard on 26th December. She was twenty-eight by this time and he was thirty-six, so they were older than

Lizzie wrote to John every week, and waited eagerly for his replies.

OPPOSITE
Each person on the boat deck that night made a life or death decision.

ABOVE
Lizzie Lawry's extended family: she is seated on the right of the front row.

most newlyweds and they didn't want to leave it any longer to start a family.

Lizzie's brother William had emigrated to the town of Fitchburg, Wisconsin, where he was working as a carpenter, and he sent back glowing reports of the pleasant location, the favourable climate and the opportunities for earning a good living. John and Lizzie decided they would join him out there, and John booked a second-class ticket on the *Titanic*'s maiden voyage. They would sail to New York, then catch a train to Chicago, and from there to Wisconsin. It would be their belated honeymoon.

Lizzie was beside herself with excitement. After all the years of waiting, her dreams of a new life, with a home and a family of her own, were about to come true. What's more, she had read that the *Titanic* was more luxurious than any ship that had ever been built. At £26 (the equivalent of £1,462/ $2,600 today) the cost of their ticket was a huge amount of money for them, but it was their one extravagance in a life that was otherwise very plain and hardworking.

Lizzie said her goodbyes to her friends and family in Cornwall, knowing that it would probably be a long time before she saw them again, and she bought little mementoes for her favourites. On the Sunday before they left, she gave a ceramic cup to a young boy called Hughie Beswetherick, who delivered her milk. On it were inscribed the words 'Think of me'.

NEW FRIENDS

John and Lizzie were impressed by the second-class accommodation on the *Titanic*. Their cabin was small but smart, with two berths, a couch and a mirrored washstand. Each berth was just wide enough for two, so they were able to snuggle up together in the lower one and sleep quite comfortably. They were even more impressed with the second-class dining room, which was 70 feet long and stretched the full width of the ship, with windows looking out to the Atlantic on either side. It was decorated in 17th-century style, with carved oak panels and a raised platform on which there was a piano. On the first day, when John and Lizzie walked in for dinner, summoned by a bugle call, they couldn't believe their eyes. Like many other second-class passengers, Lizzie thought they must have made a mistake and wandered into first class by accident.

Assuring them that they were in the right place, a saloon steward showed them to their table. The menu offered a choice of four main courses and the food was better than in any restaurant they had come across. There was pretty china – white with a blue grapevine pattern – and good-quality cutlery. For Lizzie, it was the epitome of luxury.

On that first evening aboard, they recognized another West Country accent and got talking to Jim Hocking, a painter and decorator from Devonport, who was on his way to join his brother in Connecticut, where he would be joined later by his wife and two children. The Chapmans and Hocking quickly became

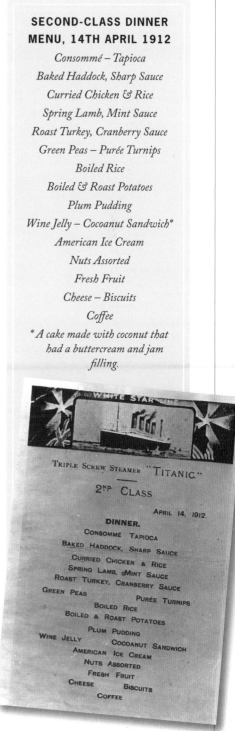

SECOND-CLASS DINNER MENU, 14TH APRIL 1912

Consommé – Tapioca

Baked Haddock, Sharp Sauce

Curried Chicken & Rice

Spring Lamb, Mint Sauce

Roast Turkey, Cranberry Sauce

Green Peas – Purée Turnips

Boiled Rice

Boiled & Roast Potatoes

Plum Pudding

Wine Jelly – Cocoanut Sandwich*

American Ice Cream

Nuts Assorted

Fresh Fruit

Cheese – Biscuits

Coffee

A cake made with coconut that had a buttercream and jam filling.

friends, and Jim wrote to his wife Ada about them in a letter he posted when the ship stopped at Queenstown: 'I have fallen in with a young couple from Liskeard named Chapman … He like myself worked for his father but could not get on with him, so I am pleased I have met someone nice, in fact, you don't meet anyone rough second class.'

The Chapmans also met Emily Richards from Penzance, who was travelling with her mother, brother, sister and two young sons to join her husband in Akron, Ohio, and Mrs Addie Wells, who was travelling with her two small children. They were all comfortably off, with good jewellery and smart clothes, and the ladies dressed up in their Sunday best for dinner each evening.

During the daytime, the Chapmans often met their new friends for a stroll on the deck, and they liked to pop into the smoking room where there was a posting showing how many miles had been covered the day before: 386 miles from Thursday to Friday, 519 from Friday to Saturday, 546 from Saturday to Sunday.

BELOW
As they strolled past the lifeboats on the boat deck, no passengers ever dreamed they would have to get into one.

Jim Hocking told them he had heard that the company wanted to make record time for the crossing, perhaps even arriving on the evening of Tuesday 16th instead of the following morning. Lizzie was disappointed to hear this, because she wanted to savour every moment of life on board. It was the most wonderful experience of her life.

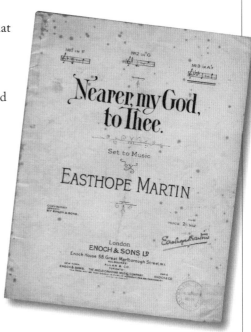

AFTER THE COLLISION

After dinner on the evening of Sunday, 14th April, John and Lizzie attended the hymn singing in the dining room, led by the Reverend E. Calder on piano. He invited the hundred-strong crowd to call out their favourite hymns. One chosen was 'For Those in Peril on the Sea'.

'We're not in peril,' the reverend said, 'but others may be. Let us sing the hymn for them.' Later, his words would resonate in the minds of survivors in a way they could never have imagined at the time.

Stewards brought around coffee and biscuits, then John and Lizzie went to bed. They were talking while in each other's arms when they felt the jolt of the collision. They were used to a slight vibration from the ship's engines and didn't think much of it, but when the engines stopped completely and they could hear the loud release of steam from the funnels, John decided to find out what was going on.

Out in the corridor, he saw people milling around, asking each other for news. Then a steward appeared and announced, 'Everyone up on deck,' instructing them to bring life-jackets.

'What's going on?' John asked.

'It's just a precaution, sir,' was the reply. 'There's been a bit of a bump but nothing to worry about.'

John and Lizzie got dressed quickly. He decided that they should bring their official papers in case they had to transfer to another ship, so he put their marriage certificate, baggage receipt and baggage insurance form into Lizzie's handbag, along with all their money – £63 10 shillings in gold, £13 7 pence in silver and copper, plus $2 in paper and silver. Perhaps he

ABOVE
Opinions differ about the last song played by the band as the ship sank. Was it 'Nearer, my God, to Thee' or 'Song d'Automne'?

ABOVE
*Second Officer Lightoller.
In press reports and
during the Senate
Inquiry, he would be
both praised for saving
lives and, paradoxically,
criticized for not filling
boats to maximum
capacity.*

suspected the collision was serious; or else he didn't want to take any risks.

They climbed the stairs on the port side of the boat and were directed by stewards into the second-class dining room, where a ladder led to the promenade on A Deck. Once they got up there, they saw Emily Richards and her party.

'We're being put into lifeboats,' Emily told them, looking shocked. 'I can't believe this is happening.'

John tried to reassure her, and his new wife, that the crew must know what it was doing.

Emily was then guided through a window into Lifeboat 4, where she huddled in the bottom of the boat with her children. Lizzie gave her handbag to John and a crewman took her by the hand and helped her down into the boat. She turned to help John into the seat beside her, before realizing he wasn't being allowed to board.

'Women and children only, sir,' Second Officer Lightoller said, holding out an arm to stop him.

Lizzie didn't hesitate. She turned to Emily: 'Goodbye, Mrs Richards. If John can't go, I won't go either.'

With that, she hauled herself back up and through the window onto the ship again. She and John sat down on the fan casing and linked arms.

Officer Lightoller came over to remonstrate with her. 'Won't you let me put you in one of the boats?' he asked.

She smiled and clutched John's arm. 'Not on your life. We started together and, if need be, we'll finish together.'

The faint sounds of the band playing drifted through the air. The atmosphere was calm and unhurried. Few people believed at that stage that they were in genuine danger, but that would change very soon.

THE LAST MOMENTS

OPPOSITE
*Under the direction of
Wallace Hartley (centre),
the orchestra continued
playing while passengers
were loaded into the
lifeboats.*

It was 1.55am when Lifeboat 4 pulled away from the *Titanic*, and by that time the bow of the ship was sinking fast into the North Atlantic. John kept hold of Lizzie's handbag as they hurried up to the boat deck to look for another lifeboat. The ship was listing so badly that they had to cling onto railings and brace themselves against walls to stay upright. When they

THE BAND PLAYED ON

Bandleader Wallace Hartley led a quintet that played at Sunday services, dinnertime and after-dinner concerts, but there was also a trio on board, who tended to play in the Café Parisien in first class. Just after midnight on 14th April, as the lifeboats were being prepared, all eight musicians assembled in the first-class lounge and began to play. Survivors recall hearing a medley of ragtime classics, but there is disagreement about the last song they played. Some claim that it was the hymn 'Nearer, my God, to Thee', while others swear it was 'Song d'Automne' by English composer Archibald Joyce. They played until about 2am, by which time there was no chance of getting into a lifeboat. All the musicians perished and, when the story of that night emerged, they were universally acclaimed as heroes. There is no doubt that their actions helped to keep passengers calm during those terrifying two hours.

looked down the stairwell, they could see water swirling below. On the boat deck, they found the davits swinging loose and all the lifeboats gone. At that stage, they both realized their chances were slim.

All around, there was an unearthly calm. They could still hear the faint sound of the band playing. Everyone was hurrying but no one was panicking and the lights continued blazing. There was no screaming or pushing, no tears or recriminations. It was all very civilized.

Just after 2am, a large crowd of third-class passengers appeared on the boat deck, having at last found their way up from below. There were still around 1,600 people on the *Titanic* and no lifeboats in sight. As the bow sank further, most tried to pull themselves up the steeply sloping deck toward the stern. The lights flickered off, then back on again. Crashing sounds could be heard from inside the ship as heavy fittings collapsed.

At around 2.15am, the ship gave a sudden lurch and a wave swept across the deck, taking many to their deaths. Those who had made it up to the stern were waiting for the right moment

THE WOMEN WHO DIED

Four women from first class and 15 from second class didn't get on to lifeboats. Ida Straus, wife of the owner of Macy's department store in New York, refused several offers, saying to her husband, 'We have lived together for many years. Where you go, I go.' Bessie Allison wouldn't get on a lifeboat because she was searching for her baby son and didn't realize his nurse had already taken him on an earlier boat. Edith Evans ushered a friend with children onto a boat but was too nervous to board herself. Ann Isham, the fourth first-class passenger, was not seen on deck after the collision and some think she chose to stay with her dog. The women from second class who refused to board either chose to stay with their husbands, or were too nervous to trust the fragile wooden craft. And of the 179 women in third class, 81 perished, most because they couldn't find their way up to the boat deck or got there too late, after the last boats had gone.

RIGHT *Ida Straus had been married to Isidor for forty-one years.*

to jump. Leaping from too high up would break their necks, but if they waited too long, they risked being sucked under as the ship went down. Each made his own decision. Single men dived or shimmied down ropes. Couples held hands and leaped. Some clung to railings, hoping against hope that the ship would somehow stay afloat. Others knelt and prayed.

TIME STANDS STILL

John's body was one of the first picked up by the *Mackay-Bennett*. He was still clutching his wife's handbag containing all the couple's official paperwork and money, and was wearing a gold watch, which had stopped at 1.45am. It's possible that he and Lizzie fell overboard at that time, while the last lifeboats were still departing, but more likely that his watch wasn't set to ship's time, which on Sunday, 14th April was one hour and 33 minutes behind New York time.

John was buried at the Fairview Lawn Cemetery in Halifax on 10th May 1912. Lizzie's body was never found. After all the years of waiting to be together, their marriage lasted only 15 short weeks.

ABOVE
A memorial to John and Lizzie was carved on her aunt's headstone in St Neot churchyard, Cornwall.

Couples held hands and leaped. Some clung to railings, hoping against hope that the ship would somehow stay afloat. Others knelt and prayed.

PASSENGER MANIFEST

3RD CLASS

Name, *John Bourke (b. May 1869).*

Name, *Kate McHugh (b. October 1879).*

Married, *17th January 1911.*

Point of embarkation, *Queenstown.*

Ticket no. *364849.*

John & Kate
Bourke

Fourteen people from the same small area of County Mayo, all family and friends, travelled together on the *Titanic*, bound for a new life in North America. Only three survived. When the news of the tragedy reached the tiny community from which they hailed, the shock was overwhelming.

The Daily Mirror

THE MORNING JOURNAL WITH THE SECOND LARGEST NET SALE.

No. 2,646.   April 17, 1912   One Halfpenny.

PASSENGERS BOARDING THE TITANIC AT QUEENSTOWN AND SOME OF THE VICTIMS AND SURVIVORS OF HISTORY'S MOST TERRIBLE SHIPWRECK.

Chief Purser McElroy (clean-shaven) and Dr. W. F. N. O'Loughlin, the chief ship's surgeon. Both are missing.   Mr. K. H. Behr, the famous tennis player, saved.   Sir Cosmo Duff-Gordon, Bart., and his wife, who is better known as "Lucile." Both of them are reported saved.

Embarking on the Titanic at Queenstown last Thursday. This was the last port at which the ill-starred vessel called.

Mr. Daniel Marvin, reported missing, and his bride, who is saved. They were on a wedding trip.   Mr. Head (missing), a prominent member of Lloyd's.   Colonel J. J. and Mrs. Astor, returning from their honeymoon. She is saved, but his body has been picked up dead.

Queenstown was the last port at which the ill-fated Titanic called. She sailed on Thursday with the good wishes of everyone, only to founder less than a week afterwards. Two young brides, Mrs. J. J. Astor, the wife of the millionaire, and Mrs.   Daniel Marvin, who had been spending their honeymoon in Europe, have been widowed by the disaster. Mr. Christopher Head was formerly Mayor of Chelsea. —(*Daily Mirror*, Dover-street Studios, and Russell.)

KATE McHUGH'S LIFE was touched by tragedy long before she set foot on the *Titanic*. One of nine children from Tawnagh, a farming village in County Mayo on Ireland's west coast, she was just seven years old when her parents died within months of each other. She was brought up by her elder sister Maria. As a young woman, in 1901, Kate emigrated to Rochdale to live with another sister, Hannah, and got work in a cotton mill.

Kate visited her siblings back home on a few occasions, and during those trips she sometimes stepped out with John Bourke of Lahardane. Bourke was a kind, straightforward farmer and she enjoyed their evenings out. However, in 1905, when her cousin, Bridget McDermott, invited Kate to Chicago, she decided to accept the offer. Kate was an adventurous type. She already had plenty of family members in Chicago, and it sounded as though America had more to offer than either Rochdale or rural Ireland. She sailed on the *Etruria* with just $15 in her pocket, arriving at Ellis Island on 16th July 1905, at the age of twenty-three.

OPPOSITE
National and local newspapers were rife with first speculation and then reports of those who had survived and those who had perished in the disaster.

BELOW
Before being allowed to disembark in New York, third-class passengers had to clear immigration on Ellis Island, just by the Statue of Liberty.

... it sounded as though America had more to offer than either Rochdale or rural Ireland.

Kate found work in Chicago and had a good life among her extended family but, perhaps because she was no great beauty, she didn't manage to get herself a husband. The anti-Irish prejudice in those days meant she would have been unlikely to attract a man from outside her own community, and her fellow countrymen all seemed to be taken.

In 1910, she decided to return to Ireland for a few months to visit relatives. Once again, she began to step out with John Bourke. By this time, she was thirty-one years old, past marriageable age in many people's eyes, while he was a bachelor ten years her senior. Maybe they realized their chances of married bliss were growing slimmer, although it seems there was a real love growing between them. They married in Saint Patrick's Church, Lahardane, on 17th January 1911, and planned to live their lives on John's farm.

However, Kate missed the excitement of life in Chicago. When another cousin, Catherine McGowan, was over visiting from the United States, she and Kate spent a lot of time reminiscing about the range of food available, the lively dance halls and the higher standard of living.

'Why don't you sell the farm and come back out?' Catherine urged. 'You could use the money to start a business of your own, and be your own bosses.' Catherine was sailing back to the United States on the *Titanic*'s maiden voyage with her fifteen-year-old niece. 'Why not come with us?' she suggested.

RIGHT
Young Kate McHugh went to America hoping for a better standard of living than she had back in Ireland or Rochdale.

John and Kate thought long and hard about the proposal, before finally deciding to go along. They thought they might start their own haulage business.

'We never had a honeymoon,' Kate reminded her husband. 'Why don't we voyage on the *Titanic*?' She'd been reading in magazines about all the luxuries on board – the Turkish bath, the gymnasium, the beautiful decor – and thought the whole idea romantic.

John was persuaded. He sold his farm and bought two third-class tickets from the local White Star Line representative, Thomas Durcan of Castlebar, for the sum of £15 10 shillings. His unmarried sister Mary decided she would accompany them.

John, Kate and Mary weren't the only ones in the area who were tempted by the fortunes they'd heard could be made in the Land of Opportunity. Apart from Catherine and her niece Annie McGowan, there was Annie Kelly of Castlebar and her cousins Patrick and Mary Canavan and James Flynn; Mary Mangan and Nora Fleming from Carrowskehine; Bridget O'Donohue and Delia McDermott from Lahardane; and Delia Mahon of Derrymartin – 14 altogether from the same parish. John and Mary were the oldest, with most of the rest being in their twenties and Annie McGowan only fifteen.

The night before they left for Queenstown to board the *Titanic*, they held a 'live wake' in Castlebar, at which hundreds of friends wished them well and toasted them on their way. It was an emotional occasion for all the guests.

LIVE WAKES

There were waves of emigration from Ireland to America in the 1850s, following the famine that had decimated the population. By the end of the 19th century, the Irish were still dependent on agriculture and endured severe hardship whenever bad weather destroyed the crops, or competition from abroad depressed prices, so emigration remained a popular option for those who could raise the fare. It was customary when anyone left for the New World to hold a farewell party, known as a live wake. These wakes were tinged with sadness because in the 19th century at least, it was unlikely that the emigrants would ever see their relatives again, given the length of the journey and the high cost of the ticket. By 1911, transatlantic travel was easier, as shown by the fact that Kate and Catherine came back for a visit. No one at the live wake in Castlebar on 10th April guessed that it really was the last time they would see their friends.

LEFT
The White Star Line logo adorned china in the third-class dining room.

BOARDING THE *TITANIC* AT QUEENSTOWN

The *Titanic* overshadowed all the other vessels in Queenstown harbour, and some of the younger girls in the party were terrified as they were rowed out to it, but Kate and Catherine were able to set their minds at rest. After all, they'd already been back and forth across the Atlantic. 'We'll have a laugh,' they said. 'You'll love it.'

The County Mayo contingent were put in cabins close to each other down in third class, well away from the Eastern Europeans who had boarded the day before at Cherbourg and who, certain other passengers complained, were filling the steerage with unwelcome smells. They spent their first days out on deck, enjoying the fresh air, and in the evenings they visited the public rooms for third-class passengers. There was a dining room on the middle deck, which extended the width of the ship and could seat 470 passengers in each sitting, as well as a general meeting room with pine wall panels, teak furniture and a piano, and a separate smoking room so that the ladies need not be subjected to pungent tobacco smoke. They made a well-dressed group, who obviously had a bit of money between them.

On the night of Sunday, 14th April, the County Mayo crowd attended a party in the meeting room, where Kate is reported to have sung 'Moonlight in Mayo'. By all accounts,

OPPOSITE
Bags of mail were loaded on board at Queenstown, and some lucky passengers disembarked there.

BELOW
The smoking room for third-class passengers had oak-panelled walls and teak benches and tables.

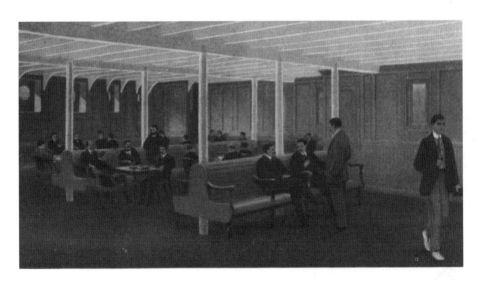

**THIRD-CLASS MEALS ON
SUNDAY, 14TH APRIL**

Breakfast
*Oatmeal Porridge & Milk
Smoked Herrings, Jacket Potatoes
Ham & Eggs
Fresh Bread & Butter
Marmalade – Swedish Bread
Tea – Coffee*

Dinner
*Rice Soup
Fresh Bread – Cabin Biscuits
Roast Beef, Brown Gravy
Sweet Corn – Boiled Potatoes
Plum Pudding, Sweet Sauce
Fruit*

Tea
*Cold Meat
Cheese – Pickles
Fresh Bread & Butter
Stewed Figs & Rice
Tea*

Supper
Gruel – Cabin Biscuits – Cheese

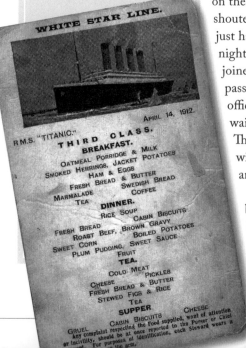

she had a beautiful singing voice. They sang and danced and were in extremely good spirits, but by 11.40pm, when the ship struck the iceberg, they had all gone to bed. The noise and motion in third class were such that few of these passengers were disturbed by the collision. However, when the ship's engines stopped and steam was released, John Bourke was prompted to wonder what was going on. He went out to find a steward, who told him that the ship had struck something, but that there was no danger.

John relayed this message to the others. Despite the steward's reassurances, they were all alarmed.

'Why don't we say a prayer?' Kate suggested. Her faith was important to her and she often recited the rosary. They got down on their knees and Kate recited the words, while the others gave the responses, each fingering his or her own set of rosary beads. This calmed them down, although they couldn't think of getting back to sleep.

Around 12.15am, a steward came knocking on their doors. 'All passengers up on deck,' he shouted. Those who hadn't dressed already just had time to pull on a coat over their nightclothes. The County Mayo party then joined a mass of people heading along the passageway towards the upper decks, but officers stopped them, saying they had to wait because they weren't ready for them. There was more of a sense of panic now, with talk of the lifeboats being launched, and the party was separated in the crush.

They had only had three days on board, which wasn't long enough to become familiar with the complex layout, but John remembered seeing ladders that led up to the boat decks.

He and Kate, along with his sister Mary, Patrick Canavan and James Flynn, hurried off to find them. Meanwhile, a steward found young Annie Kelly wandering around in her nightgown and led her up another stairway to the deck. According to Annie's later testimony, she saw some men trying to storm a lifeboat while officers brandishing guns held them back. She was petrified.

> 'I'll not leave my husband,' said Kate firmly, and she got up and jumped back on board ship.

When John and his group appeared on deck, stewards pushed Kate and Mary into Lifeboat 16. They had taken their seats when they realized that John was not going to be allowed on.

'I'll not leave my husband,' said Kate firmly, and she got up and jumped back on board ship.

'And I'll not leave my brother,' said Mary, following her without a second thought.

It was only because they didn't get on that there was space for Annie Kelly. The last time she saw the Bourkes, they were standing on deck holding onto a railing. Others reported that John Bourke and Patrick Canavan went back and helped several other third-class passengers to climb the ladders to the boat deck.

As Lifeboat 16 was rowed away, a distraught Annie Kelly watched the *Titanic* sink. She believed she was the only one of the County Mayo group to survive, but when dawn broke the next morning, she realized that Annie McGowan, the fifteen-year-old niece of Catherine McGowan, was lying nearby, also wearing only a nightgown with a coat over the top. Both teenagers were admitted to St Vincent's hospital in New York when the *Carpathia* docked, suffering from shock and exposure.

Delia McDermott was the third survivor from the County Mayo party. Despite going back to her cabin to retrieve a new hat of which she was especially fond, she was lucky enough to be helped by a steward onto Lifeboat 13. As the boat had already been lowered, she had to climb onto a rope ladder and jump down into it.

THE NEWS REACHES HOME

On 15th April, news filtered back to Ireland that the *Titanic* had collided with an iceberg. According to those early stories, it was limping into port and all passengers had been saved. While wild rumours began circulating among friends and relatives at home in Ireland, the White Star Line agent, Thomas Durcan, wired his head office in Liverpool, England, for news. The reply came back on Tuesday, 16th April:

Liverpool. 4.30pm Tuesday.
Referring to your telegram re. **Titanic,** *deeply regret to say that latest word received is steamer foundered; about 675 souls, mostly women and children saved.*

BELOW
Crowds desperate for news outside the White Star Line offices in Leadenhall Street, London.

The relatives in Lahardane were distraught, but still had hope that the women, who made up the bulk of the party of 14, had survived. On Thursday, the name of Annie McGowan appeared on a list of survivors printed in the papers, followed later by that of Annie Kelly, but, by the weekend, it seemed there weren't going to be any more following. The *Chicago*

Evening News printed a story saying that only two of the County Mayo party had survived, and commented: 'There is grief here in Chicago where relatives mourn and grief back home in Mayo over the sudden end to the dreams and plans of some of the flower of Ireland's youth.'

No mention was made of Delia McDermott. This was probably because she had stayed in New York, so the Chicago press didn't learn of her existence. It was only later that her relatives found out that she had survived, much to their overwhelming relief.

Eleven members of the original 14 had perished. The tiny village of Carrowskehine, with a population of only 61, lost not only John Bourke, who hailed from there, but five young women as well. The grief was unbearable. For two days and two nights, the town held wakes. Pure white quilts were placed on the beds the girls had slept on before they left, photos were placed on the pillows and candles were lit all around, while friends and family sat to pay their respects, barely sleeping at all, many of them overcome, breaking down and unable to control themselves.

It was said that Kate Bourke had been pregnant when she set sail. Her sister Maria didn't believe it. 'If Kate had been pregnant,' she said, 'she would have stayed put on that lifeboat to save her child.'

Everyone concurred that it was just like John Bourke to try to save others during his own last minutes of life.

Neither of their bodies was ever found. It was a tragic end to their later-in-life romance, the belated honeymoon Kate had been so excited about, and all their plans and dreams of making their fortune far across the wide ocean from their homeland.

WERE THE EXITS FROM THIRD CLASS LOCKED?

Some third-class passengers reported that when they tried to get up on deck, the way was blocked by locked gates and stewards. The suggestion is that there was a deliberate policy of giving first-class passengers priority to board the lifeboats. Certainly, the statistics would seem to bear this out. Despite the call for 'women and children first', the proportion of third-class children who died was greater than that of first-class men. The statistics might not result entirely from class prejudice. Barriers would have been kept closed between third-class and other areas of the ship, but Board of Trade requirements stated that emergency exits were not to be locked. Class barriers were necessary because of health restrictions, and because third-class passengers would have to clear immigration at Ellis Island on arrival in New York. The shipping line also wanted to prevent third-class passengers from perusing the first-class compartments. However, on the night of 14th April, it does appear that priority was given to rescuing first-class passengers. In the class-conscious society of the time, this was regarded as the natural order of things.

PASSENGER MANIFEST

3RD CLASS

Name, ... Neal McNamee (b. 29th August 1884).

Name, ... Eileen O'Leary (b. 16th December 1892).

Married, ... 17th January 1912.

Point of embarkation, ... Southampton.

Ticket no. .... 376566.

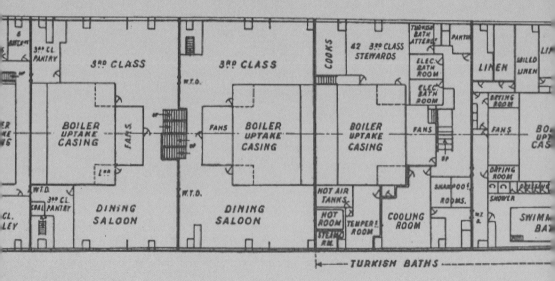

OPPOSITE

A third-class Titanic *passenger's inspection card. All third-class passengers had to pass a health check before they were permitted to board.*

Neal & Eileen McNamee

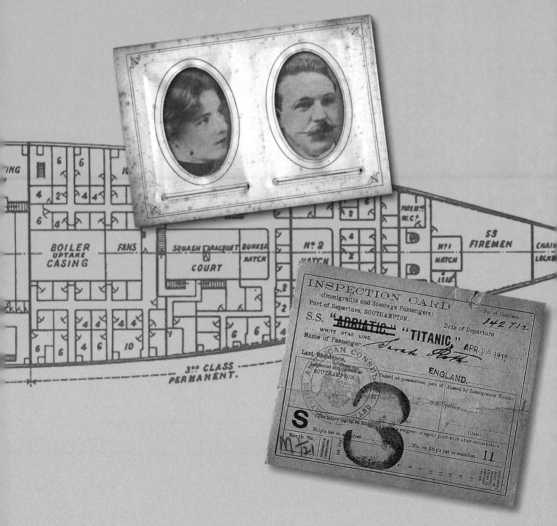

Neal and Eileen were exactly the kind of immigrants the United States wanted. He already had a good job lined up in New York, they had savings to help them set up home, and they were young and hard-working. In the Land of Opportunity, a prosperous future should have been theirs for the taking.

Neal's boss, Sir Thomas Lipton, was a self-made man. His family was from the north of Ireland but he was born and educated in Glasgow. He set off round the world, doing a number of jobs, before returning to establish the first Lipton's grocery store in 1870. He expanded the business quickly and, by 1888, he had 300 stores around the country, catering for the rising middle classes. He spotted the growing market for tea, created the Lipton's tea brand and established it throughout Europe and North America, consolidating his fortune. To young Neal McNamee, he was a hero. Neal had a burning ambition to travel and start his own business one day, exactly as Sir Thomas had done.

Eileen caught Neal's eye right away because she was a real looker.

Neal was born in the tiny village of Convoy in Donegal, Ireland, where the only industry was a woollen mill. He got a job working in Lipton's grocery in Derry and within two years his potential had been noted and he was promoted to the London branch. He was a dedicated employee, happy to move between stores, and he gained experience as the manager of several district branches. In 1910, he was provisions manager for the Salisbury area when young Eileen O'Leary applied for a cashier's job in the town branch at 41 Silver Street.

Eileen caught Neal's eye right away because she was a real looker. She had dark wavy hair, dark eyes and petite features, and she was always well dressed. She teased Neal about his Donegal accent and his showy waxed moustache, but when he asked if she would like to be his girlfriend, she was delighted. He was kind and personable, and she also admired his ambition and determination to make something of himself. It was well known in Lipton's that he was 'going places'.

When Neal proposed to Eileen, she had a difficult decision to make. He was a Catholic, but she was a committed member of Salisbury's Baptist Church, where she taught a Sunday school class. Interfaith marriage wouldn't have been acceptable

ABOVE AND OPPOSITE
Neal and Eileen had a workplace romance at Lipton's tea store in Salisbury.

COMPETITION BETWEEN THE SHIPPING LINES

The four main shipping companies that took passengers across the Atlantic were the White Star Line, Cunard, Hamburg-American and North German Lloyd. Although they were eager to attract top-paying, first-class passengers, the bread-and-butter money was in transporting the million or so emigrants per year to the United States. Unlike tourists, they travelled all year round and, along with the transport of mail, they helped to keep the shipping companies in profit. A lot of advertising for the new ships was, therefore, aimed at them. Prior to this, third-class passengers undertaking the voyage had been crammed together in a section known as steerage. They slept in huge compartments with 200 to 400 others and often caught contagious illnesses, giving the liners the nickname 'coffin ships'. However, the *Titanic* was described in advertisements as 'palatial' as well as 'affordable'. In third class, there was a choice of two-, four- or six-bed cabins, as well as a cheaper dormitory for only men, and emigrants were given a generous luggage allowance of 10 cubic feet per person.

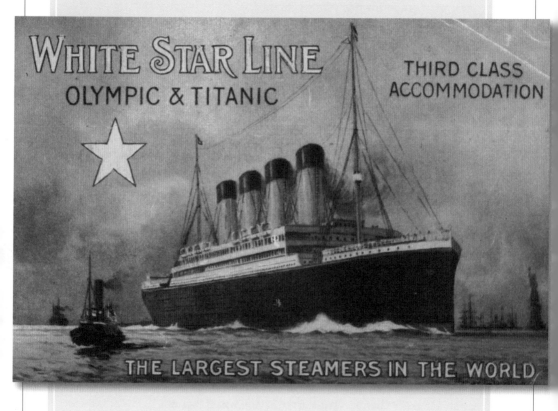

ABOVE *Thousands of emigrants arrived in New York every year on a White Star Line ship.*

in the eyes of either church, so she would have to convert to Catholicism to marry him. Not only that, he wanted to go to the United States, where he'd been offered a job at Lipton's New York store, so she would have to leave behind her family. By this stage, however, Eileen had fallen head over heels in love, so she accepted his proposal.

PREPARATIONS FOR THE JOURNEY

Neal bought a pretty turquoise and diamond engagement ring and the wedding was booked at the Corpus Christi Roman Catholic Church in Bournemouth for the following January. Meanwhile, Eileen had to take conversion classes and learn her catechism so she could be accepted into Neal's church.

'How would you feel about having your honeymoon on board the *Titanic*, while we sail to America?' Neal asked, with a grin on his face.

Eileen was surprised. 'Can we afford it?' she asked. 'Surely it will cost too much?'

'It's 16 pounds and 2 shillings for a superior cabin in third class. I saw a picture in a brochure in the White Star Line office and it looks top notch. What do you say?'

Eileen was excited. The magazines were full of advertisements for this floating palace, said to be the most attractive and comfortable of all the transatlantic ships.

Her mother, however, wasn't so happy when she heard the news. She was fearful. When Eileen was two years old, the family had sailed out to Malta in order for Eileen's father to help with the installation of a public electricity service on the island. Their boat was caught up in a hurricane and lost power, and they drifted engineless for miles in the Bay of Biscay before being rescued.

'The *Titanic* is the safest ship in the world. We'll be fine,' Eileen promised.

News reached Sir Thomas Lipton of the couple's impending journey. Neal had met Sir Thomas when he'd visited some of the stores he was managing, and he was utterly thrilled when his hero offered to write a letter of recommendation to the general manager of the New York store, saying what a talented man he was. Armed with a personal letter from the boss, Neal's future prospects looked bright.

Eileen received a letter of recommendation of her own. The mayor of Salisbury, Mr W. Pritchard, gave her a letter thanking her for all her work for the Sunday school and guaranteeing her good character, as well as a gift of a Bible. Her mother watched as she packed her trunk and recalled that the Bible was the last thing she slipped in on top.

First thing in the morning on 10th April, the couple said their goodbyes and caught a train for the short journey to Southampton. When they walked across from the station into the port, Eileen caught her breath at the sheer size of the *Titanic*, which towered like a mountain above them. It was exciting and scary at the same time.

THEIR FINAL DAYS

Neal and Eileen were assigned a neat, clean, two-berth cabin with its own porthole looking out onto the water. They enjoyed promenading on the open deck areas, gazing out to sea, or watching the other passengers playing football or jump rope games, while the children raced around after each other. One man had brought a set of bagpipes on board and his mournful tunes often filled the air.

BELOW
Third-class passengers boarded at Southampton between 9.30 and 11am on Wednesday, 10th April, and were checked by medical staff before being shown to their cabins.

The third-class dining room was like a proper restaurant, with an individual chair for each passenger instead of long communal benches. At mealtimes, they were served by smart, uniformed stewards, and the food was tasty, with plenty of soups, stews, desserts and freshly baked bread. In the meeting room, there were little tables and chairs where they could sit and write postcards, play dominoes or chat. There were also two bars for third-class male passengers: one on D Deck, near the men's dormitory, and the other near the stern on C Deck. The decor may not have been as ornate as the first-class accommodations they had seen in the brochures, but there was real wood panelling on the walls and everything was freshly painted and sparkling clean.

Eileen had read that you could send Marconi-grams home to your loved ones from the ship and wondered whether she could send one to her parents, but when Neal asked a steward he was told that it cost 12 shillings and sixpence for the first ten words and then ninepence for each additional word. It was way beyond their budget.

'Don't worry!' Eileen said cheerfully. 'I'll send a postcard instead.' Nothing could ruin her enjoyment of the trip.

In the evenings, they enjoyed listening to the piano playing and watching the Irish crowd dancing in the meeting room. Although Eileen was shy, Neal managed to persuade her to dance with him a couple of times.

On the evening of Sunday, 14th April, Eileen and Neal had returned to their cabin when the ship struck the iceberg. Whatever happened subsequently took them both to watery graves. No one reported seeing them on deck, and there are no records of what they did in the last two hours of the ship's life. It does seem that Eileen got dressed carefully. When her body was recovered, she was wearing a blue flannel petticoat with the initials E. M. C. embroidered on it, under a blue skirt with

ABOVE
A view of the second- and third-class quarters. The promenade deck for third-class passengers was often the site of an impromptu game of football.

black braid and a white sailor blouse with a blue anchor on the front. Over this she wore a brown velvet coat and had chosen black shoes. Had she made it into a lifeboat, she would have been perishing cold in this outfit. No one knows what Neal was wearing.

WHAT HAPPENED TO THE THIRD-CLASS PASSENGERS?

Some stewards looked after the passengers on their watch, knocking on their cabin doors to alert them to the unfolding disaster, while others didn't. Down on the third-class decks (E, F and G), no one seemed to feel any great sense of panic. While the lifeboats were being loaded up above, some men were even seen out on the third-class poop deck playing an improvised game of football with some chunks of ice that had been sheared off the berg during the collision.

When told that they were to be loaded into lifeboats, many third-class passengers went to pack their suitcases. Unlike the wealthier passengers upstairs, they couldn't risk losing their worldly possessions because they would never be able to

BELOW
Jack Phillips, the senior of the two Marconi operators on board, stayed at his post trying to get help for the stricken ship long after Captain Smith had given him leave to save himself.

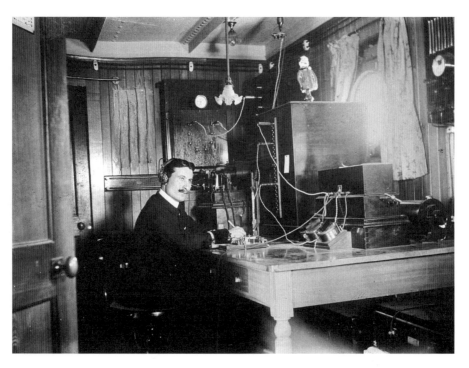

replace them. Many were seen dragging their trunks along 'Scotland Road', a wide alleyway on E Deck stretching half the length of the ship, leading from third-class up to the first-class areas, past the crew's accommodations.

The lower decks of the ship resembled a rabbit warren, full of dead ends. If they were not accompanied by a steward, third-class passengers, such as Neal and Eileen, were likely to get lost. One steward, John Hart, collected two groups of women and children and led them up to the boat deck, but few others seem to have done so. Hart took his first group of 28 at 12.25am and they arrived just in time to get onto Lifeboat 13. He went back for another group of 38 and they were loaded onto Lifeboat 15, on which he escaped himself. Thanks to Hart's efforts, these 66 third-class passengers were rescued, but Neal and Eileen were not among them.

The seriousness of the situation became apparent as the lower decks began to flood. Some third-class passengers found their own way up to the boat deck, either through the tangle of corridors or by climbing giant cranes that led up from the third-class decks. The odds of survival were stacked against them, simply because the boats left from the first-class areas of the ship and they were stuck down below. Apart from those in boats 13 and 15, 70 third-class passengers were evacuated in the collapsibles, the last boats to leave. Only 37 of them made it into the other 14 lifeboats, many of which were only half full.

Any third-class men who survived did so through sheer gritty determination and a willingness to break the rules. They broke through gates, pushed past the crew and leaped into lifeboats as they were being lowered, or they swam to a collapsible after

THE LAST WIRELESS TRANSMISSIONS

12.25am to *Carpathia*: *'Come at once. We have struck a berg. It's a CQD, OM.'* CQD was the international call meaning 'Come quickly, distress'. OM is an abbreviation for 'old man'.

12.26am to *Ypiranga*: *'Require immediate assistance. We have collision with iceberg. Sinking. Can hear nothing but noise of steam.'*

12.30am to *Frankfurt*: *'Tell your captain to come to our help. We are on the ice.'* CQD calls then received by *Olympic, Prinz Friedrich Wilhelm, Frankfurt, Mount Temple, Celtic, Caronia, Baltic, Cincinnati, Asian* and *Virginian.*

1.10am to *Olympic*: *'We are in collision with berg. Sinking head down. Come soon as possible.'*

1.25am to *Olympic*: *'We are putting the women off in the boats.'*

1.45am to *Carpathia*: *'Engine room full up to the boilers.'*

1.48am: *Asian* hears *Titanic* sending out the new SOS signal, the first time it has been used.

2am: *Virginian* hears a very faint call from *Titanic* with much reduced power.

2.17am: *Titanic*'s faint signals end abruptly as power is lost.

ABOVE
*Captain Smith took
the southward shipping
route, but he knew
there was a likelihood
of icebergs in April.*

the ship went down. Those who waited down on the lower decks, thinking that someone was bound to come and collect them and their baggage, didn't stand a chance. Afterwards, there were claims that crew members had prevented third-class passengers from reaching the boat deck, but there is no clear evidence to support this. It does seem likely that the crew didn't afford the same level of aid to third-class passengers as they did to first-class. News of the ship's demise was too late to reach many third-class passengers, who stayed below waiting for instruction.

Neal and Eileen seem to have made it up onto the boat deck, because her body was found in the open water and didn't go down with the ship.

BACK HOME IN BRITAIN

As news of the *Titanic*'s sinking broke, Neal's parents in Donegal and Eileen's in Salisbury could only pray. By Thursday, 18th April, the list of survivors had been received but their children's names weren't on it. They hoped there had been some mistake. It was only on Friday, 19th April, knowing the *Carpathia* had docked the night before, that they had to accept that the newlyweds had perished. A wire from New York confirmed this was the most likely scenario. Sir Thomas Lipton immediately sent his condolences, and the manager of Lipton's store in New York did the same.

On Monday, 22nd April, news came through that Eileen's body had been recovered by the *Mackay-Bennett*. She had been wrapped in her brown velvet coat and holding her handbag,

SURVIVAL RATES

	SURVIVORS	TOTAL ON BOARD	PERCENTAGE SAVED
First-class passengers	203	325	62.5
Second-class passengers	118	285	41.4
Third-class passengers	178	706	25.2
Crew	212	908	23.3
Totals	**711**	**2,224**	**32.0**
First-class men	57	175	32.6
Third-class men	75	462	16.2
First-class women	140	144	97.2
Third-class women	76	165	46.0
First-class children	6	6	100.0
Third-class children	27	79	34.2

Figures from British Parliamentary Papers, 1912. Note that figures differ across sources, so no one can say for sure exactly how many survived. This report, for example, does not take into account Helen Loraine Allison, the first-class child who died.

which contained their tickets, a fountain pen, a key, some cosmetics and a purse containing one shilling and eleven pennies. A crewman wrote of the bodies they picked up, 'I expected to see the poor creatures very disfigured but they all look as calm as if they were asleep.'

Eileen was buried at sea. Neal's body wasn't found. It was a shocking waste of two young lives with all their potential. They would never create a home together, and never have children or grandchildren. All that was left was a memorial plaque and bench for them in a Salisbury park, with a tree planted alongside.

'*I expected to see the poor creatures very disfigured but they all look as calm as if they were asleep.*'

The author and picture researcher would like to thank the following for their assistance with research: Karel Bata, Robert Bracken and Charles Haas of the Titanic International Society, Sheila Brogan, Yoshiko and Eddie Dalal, James C. Frauenthal, Alan Hustak, Baynon McDowell of the New York Hospital for Joint Diseases, Dee McMath, Chris Timms. Please note that the work does not necessarily represent their opinions.

Picture credits:

Akg-images: 32–33, 40, 73, 140–141,153; North Wind Picture Archives: 113; Ullstein bild: 184; Universal Images Group: 90L

Jayne Ansell: 105

Robert Bracken: 105L&R, 107, 115, 155TL

Sheila Brogan: 167,170,

Corbis: Bettmann: 55, 60, 68, 82, 99; Hulton-Deutsch Collection: 92; Todd Gipstein RMS Titanic, Inc: 117; Underwood & Underwood: 127

John P. Eaton-Charles A. Haas: 179L&R, 180T&B

John Frost Historical Newspapers: 124, 161, 168, 188

Getty Images: Boyer/Roger Viollet: 94; FPG/Hulton Archive: 129; Hulton Archive: 6, 15, 98, 125; Mansell/Time & Life Pictures:156; Topical Press Agency/Hulton Archive: 164

Hennepin County Library: 130, 132 T&B

Huntington Quarterly: 116L&R, 118

Alan Hustak: 51TL&TR, 52, 53

iStock: 22, 34, 90C

Library of Congress: 8, 9, 14, 23R, 25, 26, 27, 35, 38T, 38B, 41, 44, 45, 46L, 47, 48, 63, 77T, 78, 79, 101,103TL, BC, BR, 106T&B, 111, 122, 145, 146, 162,169

Liverpool and London Steamship Protection and Indemnity Association: Images provided by National Museums Liverpool, 65B, 143L

Mary Evans Picture Library: 39, 54, 69, 71, 100, 120-121, 126, 131; *Illustrated London News*: 17, 43, 90R, 122 inset, 135, 149, 185; Onslow

Auctions Ltd: 6TL,11, 56–57, 114, 139, 147, 173, 182; Rue des Archives/Tallandier: 163;

Museum of Southwestern Michigan College: 37, 46R, 49

National Archives of New York City: 152

NYU Hospital for Joint Diseases Archives, NYU Langone Medical Center, New York, New York: Original source, Philip Gowan 65T, 66, 75

Gill Paul: 36, 104

Rex Features: CSU Archives/Everett Collection: 6, 10, 29, 160; Stanley Lehrer Collection: 59

Rochester Democrat & Chronicle: 143R, 144

SWNS.com: 155B

Thinkstock: 103BL, 166–67

Chris Timms: 155TR,158,165

Titanic Historical Society: 22–23

Topfoto: 2, 12, 23L, 30, 61, 62, 93T, 95, 96, 109, 112, 133, 136, 172, 176, 180;

The Granger Collection: 13, 77B, 81, 85, 119; National Pictures: 174, 179B; PA Photos: 86; Public Record Office/HIP: 16; Roger-Viollet: 19, 81T&B, 88, 186; Ullsteinbild: 24, 84 ,87 120T,159; UPPA: 51BR, 58, 171; Charles Walker: 108;

Every effort has been made to acknowledge pictures used in this publication. We apologize if there are any unintentional omissions.

A note on money equivalents

To get a rough idea of the 21st-century equivalent of a 1912 price in British pounds, multiply by 56.25. To convert 1912 British pounds to contemporary US dollars, simply add two zeros; so £13, the cost of a second-class ticket for one, becomes $1,300. Keep in mind that these conversions don't account for the fact that money was harder to come by for the poor in 1912 than it is now. It would take years of scrimping for a factory worker to save £13, or this sum might have been completely out of reach. For the richest passengers on the *Titanic*, however, their first-class tickets represented mere loose change.